Pedlars' Guide To The Great Outdoors

Pedlars' Guide To The Great Outdoors

Charlie and Caroline Gladstone, Kate Burt

Illustrations by Matt Blease
Photography by Tim Winter

◼ SQUARE PEG

Published by Square Peg 2012

2 4 6 8 10 9 7 5 3 1

First published in Great Britain in 2012 by
Square Peg
Random House, 20 Vauxhall Bridge Road,
London SW1V 2SA

www.vintage-books.co.uk

Addresses for companies within The Random House Group Limited can be found at:
www.randomhouse.co.uk/offices.htm

The Random House Group Limited Reg. No. 954009

A CIP catalogue record for this book
is available from the British Library

ISBN 9780224095433

Typeset and designed by Mercy
www.mercyonline.co.uk

Printed and bound in Italy by Graphicom

*To Jack, India, Tara, Xanthe, Kinvara and Felix with all
deepest love and thanks for still wanting to play with us*

INTRODUCTION

Charlie: Once, when our daughter India was at primary school she was asked to draw her parents doing something they loved. She drew us standing by a bonfire and underneath she wrote, 'Mummy and Daddy like being outside. When they are out they don't want to come inside.' That was spot on.

I grew up in the countryside in Wales and my parents, I think, considered time indoors to be time wasted. Many of the very best bits of my childhood were spent outside on our annual summer holidays in Scotland. When we were there, our parents would forget about us (in a good way) and let us run wild. We spent days building rafts that then sank, making dens, swinging from bridges, falling into the river, fishing and playing complicated, but brilliant, make-believe games. We loved camping on the tiny island in the lake near our holiday house, and we tried and tried (and sometimes succeeded) to trap rabbits. We learnt how to skin the rabbits and cooked them on a spit on a campfire. We loved foraging for wild blueberries (or blaeberries, as they are called in Scotland, where we live) and even trying to pan for gold in the River Dye, which runs close to the house where we'd spend our holidays – and where we now live. Once we even built a miniature fish farm and tried to sell our stock of sticklebacks to our parents' friends; they weren't interested.

We'd stay outside until after dark, we did some unbelievably reckless, dangerous things and we were often eaten alive by midges. But those times in the great outdoors shaped me, and thinking about them today makes my heart race. I don't mind if it pours with rain, or blows a gale or chucks hail at me. And I'm equally happy if it's dark. I just like the feeling of being outside.

These are big, bold memories and there are loads of them. Equally, there are loads of similarly important memories of time spent just wandering around in the 'great outdoors', often alone; walking the dogs, looking for mushrooms, thinking, looking at stuff. I find it hard to explain the sort of peace that I used to find at these times; the sort of peace I still do find sometimes when I am outside. For me, being outside beats everything. It helps ward off stress and fight away anxiety; it aids my thinking, heals my headaches, makes things better.

Caroline: Although my earlier childhood was spent in Paris – my father was a diplomat – I am a country girl at heart. As a child, horses were my thing and they still are today, only more so. And I have added dogs and chickens and walking to my list of things I love in the country. My happiest childhood memories come from long summers spent on the French coast; swimming, building sandcastles, beach combing, all those lovely things. Later, we moved back to the English

countryside where I spent much of my spare time riding, or wishing I was riding. Not much put me off, not even when a speeding pony galloped through an orchard and I broke my nose on a low-hanging branch. Our daughters' passion for all things equine comes from me.

Charlie and I got married when we were pretty young and our eldest child, Jack, was born in south London. But six months later, we decided that we wanted to bring up our children in the countryside and so we moved 500 miles north, to Kincardineshire, pretty much in the middle of nowhere. This makes it sound easy. Actually it wasn't entirely easy; we had no local friends when we arrived, our house was nearly derelict and we were cut off from civilisation for several weeks in our first winter. But it was definitely the right move for us, and, more than 20 years later, it's easy to see that bringing our six children up in the wilds of Scotland has been a good thing for them. But of course I'm biased – though it's hard not to feel proud when I watch one of them confidently tear up the hill on what seems like a very wild horse, or when another presents me with a freshly caught fish for the campfire that the youngest has competently helped Charlie to build. I like to think that having skills like that – and the ability to create entertainment without a computer or TV screen – is a good thing. (Though, very occasionally, I do get a flash of the fear that my own parents must have felt when I was riding runaway ponies.)

Now, at Glen Dye, as well as six children we have horses and chickens and lots of dogs. And we have bridges to swing from and woods to build dens in and our children have grown up running (just a little bit) wild. We spend our free time together, walking and camping and building fires, playing outdoor games and chopping stuff up in the great outdoors. And we know that this has had a profound effect on who our children are; it has given them confidence and peace and made them healthy and strong.

Charlie & Caroline: It is this side of our life that has led us to write this book. Over the last 20 years or so, we have both learnt a lot about being outside. Caroline has developed into an incredible campfire cook and possibly the most organised camper in the British Isles. I am pretty good with a campfire and have developed a bit of a thing for axes. We haven't set out to create a definitive guide to life outside, rather to write about the things that we've learnt by spending as much time as we possibly can outdoors. Everything here comes from us (or from our friends). Some of it is practical, some of it is life-affirming, and some of it is even perhaps a little dangerous. Whatever, we hope that it acts as a useful and engaging guide to the great…Great Outdoors.

GOOD STUFF TO KNOW

Notes

COMMON BRITISH CROPS

~ CAROLINE ~

Ever wondered what's growing in that patchwork of fields that characterises the British rural landscape? Chances are it's one of the five most common British crops.

I lived my early childhood in cities all across the globe, but teenage holidays were always spent in a village on the borders of Hertfordshire and Essex. Autumn brought golden fields of ripening wheat and barley, and I loved the feeling of hulling an ear of wheat between my hands and then chewing the raw kernels. The barley didn't taste nearly as nice though, and the barley 'awns', or spikes, can give you a nasty cut if you run them between your fingers the wrong way. The crop fields were good for hiding in too; the day my O-level results dropped through the letterbox, I grabbed the envelope and took off on a two-hour walk. Eventually, I could no longer avoid the unavoidable and sought the refuge of the ripening barley in which to open the envelope.

The jewel in the crop-foraging crown was the peas; sweet and tasty, straight from the plant. Part of the delight was the fear that the local farmer might catch us at any moment, as the pea plants didn't afford the same cover as the wheat or barley. I love the scent of both potato flowers and pea flowers wafting through the air on a warm breeze and, in the way that smells can, those scents will always take me back to the fields around Saffron Walden and Widdington. However, the smell of oilseed rape, as pungent as the yellow of the flowers is violent, is not a nice one and one that I associate with the onset of hay fever and summer colds.

A cautionary note, although it is common sense: never walk across a field that has been planted, or across the crop once it has grown, unless you want a very angry farmer after you. This is his livelihood.

~ Wheat ~

Fields of wheat are a familiar sight in all areas of Britain and there is evidence of the grain being cultivated as far back as Roman times, at least. Each stalk, topped with a tight cluster of very plump kernels and a short, bristly spike at the tip, grows to between 60 and 120cm high. Every year, the dark brown velvet of early spring-ploughed fields soon sprouts a carpet of vibrant green which grows taller through the late spring. The kernels begin to form at the end of each stalk in early summer, and by early autumn, the wheat has ripened to a pale gold and is ready for harvesting. In roll the combine harvesters, the wheat is cut, the kernels are stripped from the stalks and the stalks discarded in the fields. The stalks are then baled and the straw is used for animal bedding, and sometimes for fodder for cattle and sheep. Until 1993 (when the practice was banned in England and Wales; in Scotland it is discouraged), the stubble that was left behind in the fields was routinely burnt, and that smell of burning stubble, like the smell of bonfires, encapsulates all things autumnal. Nowadays the stubble is more likely to be ploughed back into the ground.

~ Barley ~

Summer breezes blowing through ripening fields of barley: a cinematic image that conjures images of long, lazy childhood summer holidays.

HAY OR STRAW? Do you know the difference between hay and straw? Lots of people get them confused, so in case you're one … straw is coarse and bright yellow and made from dried wheat and barley stalks; hay is dried grass, dull green in colour and softer than straw and smells sweeter.

Barley has the same growing and harvesting season as wheat and is similar in appearance, except that its kernels end in a long spike, or awn, and each head droops, rather than standing to attention as wheat does. Barley flour is used in bread production, and barley flakes are a common addition to muesli. Pearl barley, which is barley that has had the husk and bran removed, is often used in hearty winter soups and stews. However most barley produced in Britain is used either for animal feed, or in the production of beer and ale. Barley straw is used for animal bedding, although horse owners prefer wheat straw because horses tend to eat barley straw.

~ Oilseed rape ~

Although oilseed rape has been a common crop in Europe for 4,000 years, it was rarely seen in British fields until the 1970s when it exploded into the countryside in a blinding acid-yellow flash. The pungent smell of the flowering rape in late April to early May announces the start of the hay fever season for many unhappy sufferers. Once the flowers die back, the dull grey-green plants are left until the crop is harvested in the autumn, and used for animal fodder and processed into vegetable (rapeseed) oil for cooking. Interestingly, it is also increasingly being processed for use as biodiesel.

~Potatoes~

You can tell when a spring field is being prepared for a potato crop by the wide, straight ridges and furrows that cross a harrowed field as regular as lines on a piece of paper. Originating in the Andes, the potato has been a popular British crop since the late 1500s, when sailors brought maize and potatoes back from their voyages to Peru and Chile. Potato plants are herbaceous perennials that grow to about 60cm high, and have a white, pink, red, blue or purple flower with a yellow stamen and a very distinctive sweet scent. The flowers die back as the potatoes start to grow underground, and most potato harvesting is done in the late autumn. In Scotland, the October half-term school holiday is known as the 'tattie holidays', because traditionally school children were let out of school to help their parents with the potato harvest.

~ Peas ~

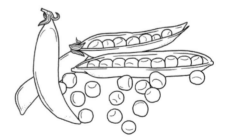

The first evidence of peas in Britain is after the Norman Conquest, although they were grown by the Greeks and Romans long before that. And, although they are one of the most commonly eaten vegetables in Britain nowadays, during Queen Elizabeth I's reign they were imported from Holland and were so expensive, they were considered a great delicacy. Until the 18th century, people mostly ate dried peas, in soups and stews, until an amateur plant breeder from Salisbury developed the first sweet-tasting pea, now known as the English pea. And so the culinary fashion for eating fresh peas took off. When you see a field of peas, they will be the low-growing variety, whereas most peas grown in vegetable gardens are the vining variety grown on a supporting trellis. Pea plants are herbaceous annuals that flower in late spring with a gorgeous and sweet-smelling flower. The flowers die back and in their place grow the pea pods that are then harvested once the peas have grown to a respectable size. Most peas harvested nowadays are frozen within a couple of hours of picking, but there is nothing like the sweet explosion of a fresh raw pea in your mouth: a just reward for the tedious but strangely therapeutic task of shelling a mountain of fresh pods.

COMMON BRITISH CATTLE

~ CAROLINE ~

'Cows are amongst the gentlest of breathing creatures; none show more passionate tenderness to their young when deprived of them; and, in short, I am not ashamed to profess a deep love for these quiet creatures.'
Thomas de Quincey

These are five of the most common types of cattle you are likely to see grazing contentedly, or lying down, lazily chewing the cud, in fields across Britain. But beware, if they are lying down, it usually means it is going to rain (see our section on predicting the weather, p.27). This old country wives' tale, like most, is grounded in truth. The cattle lie down when they sense a change in weather, so that the patch of ground they lie on is dry. Not so stupid!

~ Friesian ~

Friesians originate from the lush pastures of northern Holland and were imported to the east coast ports of England and Scotland during the 19th century. The Friesian is predominantly a dairy breed and its classic black and white markings have come to epitomise the dairy cow.

~ Hereford ~

Native to Britain as its name would suggest, the Hereford has kept its distinctive white face and red coat throughout its history, which dates back to Roman Britain. Hereford cattle are famously docile, and their meat famously tasty.

~ Charolais ~

From the Charolais region of Burgundy in France, and brought to Britain in the 1950s, the Charolais is distinctive because of its creamy coloured coat. It is a stocky, muscular animal and the calves have especially appealing faces and big sticky-out ears like a lamb's.

~ Jersey ~

Jerseys originate from the Channel island of Jersey and are renowned as a dairy breed, second only to the Friesian. They are comparatively small with a typically light, mousey-brown coat, although the colour can range from grey to a dull black. True Jerseys will always have black feet and a black nose in a white muzzle. The Jersey is the archetypal pretty cow, with big brown long-lashed eyes, and the famously rich, slightly yellow milk they produce has long been associated with luxury.

~ Highland ~

No cattle list would be complete without the Highland, originating in the Highlands and Western Isles of Scotland, but now found all over Britain. With its thick, shaggy, light-brown (dun) or black coat and majestically long sweeping horns, the Highland has become as emblematic of Scotland as the thistle or a bottle of whisky.

HOW NOT TO GET CHASED BY A COW

Hoping for a definitive answer, a friend of ours once asked a cattle farmer whether it is best to run or stand still if a herd of cows is after you. His reply was less helpful than she had hoped: 'Sometimes I stand, and sometimes I run like hell.' So, from the expert, it would appear that there are no hard and fast rules. What is true however is that cattle, cows as well as the more traditionally dangerous bulls, can be very aggressive, especially if you get between a cow and her calf. And cattle do not like dogs. So our advice is to walk round the edge of a field of cattle rather than right through the middle of it, and remember that your dog can run much faster than either the cow or you!

COMMON BRITISH CATTLE

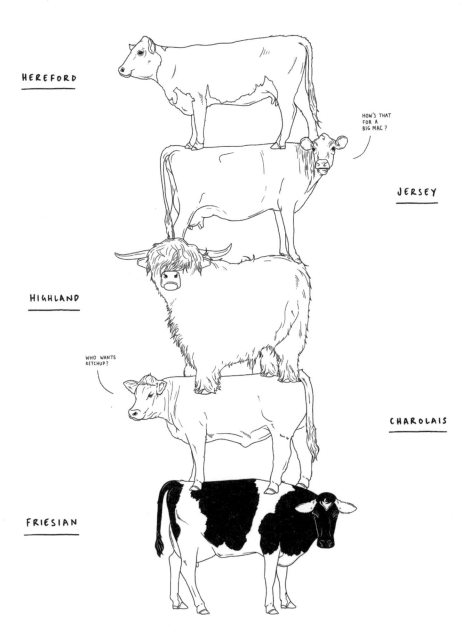

HEREFORD

HOW'S THAT
FOR A
BIG MAC?

JERSEY

HIGHLAND

WHO WANTS
KETCHUP?

CHAROLAIS

FRIESIAN

COMMON BRITISH TREES

~ CAROLINE ~

'As the poet said, "Only God can make a tree," probably because it's so hard to figure out how to get the bark on.' **Woody Allen**

~ Oak ~
Quercus

The native oak tree is one of our favourite trees, for all the very obvious reasons. The oak represents the very essence of the British countryside. It is the king of the broadleaved trees, whose strong, majestic and steadfast image is buried deep in our national psyche. It is also one of the longest living British trees, spanning several generations.

Unsurprisingly then, the oak is a symbol of strength and endurance in European folklore, and was sacred to the ancient Greeks, the Norse and the Celts. Homer's *Odyssey* associates the tree with Zeus, the 'god of gods', while in eighth-century Germany, it was the felling of 'Thor's Oak', by St Boniface, that is said to have sparked Christianity there, Thor being the Norse god of thunder. (The fact the Nordic deity was silent in the face of this destruction was Boniface's proof that Thor didn't exist.) Oaks were venerated by the Druids, who burnt their wood as a midsummer sacrifice. Indeed the word druid comes from the Latin for oak.

In more modern history, Charles II is said to have hidden in an ancient oak at Boscobel to escape the Roundheads. And according to the Robin Hood legend, 'Major Oak' is where Robin and his band of merry men sheltered: you can still visit the huge, 800-year-old tree today. More recently, every school in Lincolnshire planted an oak for the Queen Mother's 80th birthday.

The oak is the most common tree in central and southern British broadleaved woods. It is a flowering, deciduous hardwood that grows relatively slowly, and as tall as 40m, although the average is nearer 15-20m. The flowers are catkins and appear in the spring. An oak will only start to fruit, or produce acorns, when it is about 50 years old; these, in their distinctive cups, ripen from green to brown and fall in the early autumn. The tree's dark and generally green leaves have a distinct rounded finger shape, and usually come out in mid-May. The tree itself looks so distinctive it almost defies description. Loosely speaking, its shape is an upside-down, round-bottomed cone. The bark is grey with knobbly ridges.

Traditionally, there have been four main uses for the oak tree. Chiefly it is prized for its hard timber, while its bark is used for tanning leather, its acorns for fattening pigs and, because oak is long-burning, it is also used for firewood and for smoking meats. Oak barrels are still used for maturing whisky and wine.

~ Horse chestnut ~
Aesculus hippocastanum

For most British children, the horse chestnut is identifiable by its glossy, deep reddish-brown nuts, or conkers, which come hidden inside green, spiky shells. These appear in the autumn and are the sure sign that the long, languorous summer school holidays are over, and the new school year has started.

The 'conker tree' arrived in Britain during the reign of Elizabeth I, transported from south-eastern Europe. What's said to be the most ancient horse chestnut in the world, at least 2,000 years old, still grows at the base of Mount Etna in Sicily.

But the tree is not just famed for its longevity; it is also good-looking, particularly when in blossom during the spring and early summer. A flowering deciduous broadleaf, it typically grows to around 15–28m and sprouts huge upright spikes of white blooms, up to an amazing 20cm tall. These are often called candles because of their shape. The green leaves, which burst out of a sticky bud, have a distinctive hand-like form, with five to seven leaflets attaching to a stalk, like fingers to a hand.

The tree's ornamental attributes mean it has historically been planted to line avenues all over the country. And in some parts of the country 'Chestnut Sunday' is still celebrated in early May; this tradition began in the early 1900s, when people would gather to admire the blossom and picnic under the trees. Confusingly, though, the horse chestnut tree does not belong to the same family as the sweet chestnut (the name is thought to have arisen simply because conkers and chestnuts are similar-looking).

The horse chestnut's bark is smooth and grey-brown, and the twigs are a red-grey with stems that have a horseshoe-shaped mark left by the previous year's leaves.

It is a tree with little practical use, as the timber is weak and doesn't burn well. But its fruit is well loved: children have been playing conkers since at least the mid 19th century (the first record of the game in Britain was 1848, on the Isle of Wight), favouring them over cobnuts or snail shells, originally used for the same purpose (see p.104 for more on playing conkers). And conkers have other uses too, in shampoos, to add a glossy sheen to the hair, and as a herbal medicine to treat circulatory problems and varicose veins.

~ Sweet chestnut ~
Castanea sativa

A mature sweet chestnut can grow to 20–30m high, with wide, hollow trunks big enough for more than one person to squeeze into. Brilliant for an outdoor game of sardines!

The tree is valued for its weather-resistant timber; it's a similar golden colour to oak, but cheaper and more durable. But we probably know it best for its delicious, edible seeds, or chestnuts; something the Romans were already on to when they introduced the tree to Britain 2,000-odd years ago (legend would have it that Roman soldiers were given chestnut porridge before going into battle).

Other distinguishing features include oval, dark green leaves, up to 20cm long in mature trees; these have a serrated edge, a bit like a saw, and a pointed tip. The bark is silvery-purple and young trees have vertical cracks; as they age, these develop into a network of knobbly, helter-skelter-like swirls. It is a flowering deciduous broadleaf with both male and female flowers: the male flowers are catkins, which look a bit like hairy, golden caterpillars; the female flowers are like green rosettes; both appear in midsummer. By mid autumn, the female flowers develop into green spiny cases, which form a protective shell around two to four chestnuts. These ripen and fall in mid- to late October.

Raw chestnuts are not very nice but, as those Romans knew, once they have been roasted and peeled they are sweet, nutty and delicious. Who can resist buying a newspaper cornet of piping hot roasted chestnuts on a freezing winter afternoon? But better still is collecting a basketful yourself on a winter's walk, putting a cross in the top and roasting them on a chestnut roaster or a bit of tinfoil in the fire. Chestnuts are used in cakes and puddings, but they also make the boring Brussels sprout into a more interesting dish, especially with the addition of a bit of bacon or pancetta. Chestnuts can also be ground into flour and have even been used as a coffee substitute . . . though they're not much good if you need a shot of caffeine.

~ Beech ~
Fagus sylvatica

The common beech is the tree you are most likely to see with the likes of 'I luv U 4eva' carved into its trunk. But why?

This large, flowing deciduous broadleaf has particularly soft bark, making it perfect for some penknife action. But love-struck modern teenagers weren't the first to discover this quality. The word 'book' probably comes from the ancient English *bōc*, meaning 'beech', which was once used to make writing tablets.

Although the tree is now common across the whole of Britain, it is only native to southern England and south Wales. And abundantly so, many hundreds of years ago, at least: Burnham Beeches, the ancient 540-acre woodland just outside London, once covered almost the entire county of Buckinghamshire.

Its popularity elsewhere in the country is down to the tree's appearance: thanks to its somewhat stately look, a beech became the fashionable thing for 17th-century landowners to grow on their private estates. Latterly, it also became a popular ornamental feature in parks, and many beech forests were planted nationwide.

The common beech can reach a height of 40m, although more commonly it reaches between 15 and 30m, and the tree can span many generations. It flowers in April to May, producing both male and female flowers. Male catkins hang like delicate green tassels from the end of twigs, and the female flowers are four-lobed scaly cups which turn woody and form the case around the beechnuts in autumn. The beechnuts make a wonderful autumn feast for mice, voles, birds and squirrels. The dark-green leaves are small, oval and smooth-edged, turning a glorious burnt orange in autumn. The bark is smooth and grey, with occasional horizontal etchings.

Beechwood burns extremely well and is often used to smoke herrings. Otherwise the timber is used for furniture, veneers and laminates and, because it is odourless, it is also used for making cooking utensils such as wooden spoons, wooden platters and bowls.

~ London plane ~
Platanus x hispanica

As its name suggests, the London plane is the tree of the capital's streets, over which it reigns resilient and apparently unaffected by its urban circumstances. The origins of this London landmark are unclear: it may be a variety of the Western plane, or a hybrid of the Western plane and the Eastern plane, either natively occurring in Britain, or brought here from Spain.

Whatever its origins, this deciduous broadleaf first appeared in Britain in the mid 17th century and was planted as an ornamental tree, soon becoming a common urban sight. The London plane sheds its bark in great sheets, revealing the characteristic green-brown-yellow mottled pattern of its wood. This regular cycle means that the tree discards a build-up of pollutants and is kept healthy, which is why it fares so well in London and other city environments.

The tree grows to a height of between 18 and 35m, unless it is pollarded. It is surprisingly long-lived, with many trees reaching 200 years old or more. The deep-green leaves are thick, leathery and hand-shaped, with five triangular lobes. The yellowy-orange fallen autumn leaves are annually used by schoolchildren for making autumn leaf collages and crayon rubbings, because they don't dry up as quickly as many autumn leaves do. Its distinctive pom-pom seedballs hang on the trees throughout winter, releasing dandelion-like seeds in the spring; beautiful, but dreaded by sufferers of asthma and hay fever.

~ Rowan or mountain ash ~

Sorbus aucuparia

The rowan is one of Britain's most adaptable trees; it will grow pretty much anywhere. Which is partly where the 'mountain' pseudonym comes from: though it would thrive in a central London street, it is also able to grow at a higher altitude than any other tree in Britain, and does so up to 1,000m in parts of the Highlands.

You'll see rowans all over Scotland, but look out for them in other parts of Britain too, particularly the north and west. It is an attractive, slender tree with creamy-white flowers in the spring, and its characteristic bright red berries are the tell-tale sign that winter is on its way. These also make it a popular ornamental tree, especially in parks.

The rowan is a native deciduous broadleaf which grows fast, and up to a height of 8–15m, but does not live very long. The leaves are very similar to the ash (the other reason for its nickname), and are usually 15 pairs of leaflets with a single one at the tip. Each leaflet is about 5cm long, with small serrations round the edge. Bright green in the spring, they turn a glorious orange in autumn before falling off. The flowers grow in clusters, like elderflowers, and these turn into clusters of bright-scarlet to orangey-yellow berries in the autumn (see p.173 for a recipe for rowanberry jelly). The birds love the berries and I have to compete hard with them when I choose the right moment to make my jelly. The bark is greyish silver with dark, horizontal markings.

Superstition and folklore are old friends of the rowan tree. Though the tree's strong wood is used to make hardy things such as tool handles and planks or, more traditionally, cartwheels and walking sticks, it was also once used to make crosses to hang above doorways and ward off evil spirits. In Ireland, rowans were planted near houses to do the same job. In Celtic mythology, the rowan is called the 'traveller's tree' because of its supposed power to protect and guide those on long journeys. In Wales, they were planted in churchyards to prevent spirits from haunting. In Scotland, it was considered very bad luck to cut down a rowan because of the protective power that a growing tree afforded. The power was said to come from the red berries, as red was considered to be the best colour for fighting off evil spirits. According to the old wives' tale, a bumper crop of rowanberries foretells a harsh winter to come.

~ Larch ~

Larix decidua

The common, or European larch is the only deciduous conifer native to Europe and was introduced to Britain in the mid 1600s as an ornamental tree. For many of us, the larch is synonymous with the changing seasons, heralding spring with its vibrant green shoots, and announcing the onset of winter with the carpet of golden needles it sheds.

It has long been associated with Scotland, since the 18th century when several Dukes of Atholl spent 100 or so years planting around 27 million conifers across Perthshire (according to some excellent folklore, by firing the trees' seeds from cannons).

Why were they so keen? The first of the so-called 'Planting Dukes' had discovered the larch was a rampant timber tree, growing as much as 10cm a week in the hottest months of the year. This, of course, meant the trees could be felled – and sold – in about half the time it took for a native hardwood to reach the same size. The business nous of successive dukes effectively shaped the Perthshire landscape now often nicknamed 'big tree country'.

Despite the 'big tree' tag, the larch only grows between 12 and 30m tall, so it is no giant. Its soft, thin needles are a vibrant grass green in spring, turning darker over the summer and, finally, a golden yellow in the autumn before falling off. In the spring, the leaf bud is a pretty little pink cone shape. The bark is pinky-brown with wide, criss-crossing ridges and the fruit is a straw-coloured cone, which turns darker as winter draws in.

Larch timber is highly valued as it is virtually rot-proof and doesn't warp or split in wet conditions, making it ideal for use in yacht building, and for outdoor furniture, cladding, fencing . . . and hurling through the air. No Highland Games would be complete without a 'tossing the caber' competition and traditionally, the caber is a long larch pole, about 6m long and weighing about 80kg. One episode of Monty Python's Flying Circus featured the larch in the 'How to recognise different types of trees from quite a long way away' sketch. And more recently, in Harry Potter, larch is prized as a good wood for making powerful wands.

CLIMBING A GATE

~ Good gate manners ~

This may be blindingly obvious, but it is worth reiterating that if you want to scale a gate, there is a right way of doing it in order to prevent damaging it.

Climb as close as you can to the hinges, and definitely only one person at a time (the swing of some of the gates on our farm have been wrecked by adults climbing them at the opening end).

Better still, go *through* a gate, or over a stile, if you can.

TOP TEN GARDEN BIRDS

~ CHARLIE ~

'Growing up, my mom always claimed to feel bad when a bird would slam head-first into our living room window. If she "really" felt bad, though, she'd have moved the bird feeder outside.' **Rich Johnson**

I wish I knew more about garden birds. I keep trying to learn which is which, but then I get muddled. Having said that, one of our greatest pleasures is watching the birds feed on our bird table at home in Scotland. You don't need to be an expert to marvel at their variety, agility and, often, tenacity. If you haven't got a bird table, you should try one. If you haven't got a garden, a balcony window box will do; the feeding space doesn't have to be large as birds have an extraordinary knack for finding food. In freezing weather, offer them water too.

TOP TEN GARDEN BIRDS

CHAFFINCH

COAL TIT

CUCKOO

HOUSE MARTIN

FIELDFARE

GOLDCREST

BLACKBIRD

SWALLOW

ROBIN

BLUE TIT

PREDICTING THE WEATHER

'Sunshine is delicious, rain is refreshing, wind braces us up, snow is exhilarating; there really is no such thing as bad weather, only different kinds of good weather.' **John Ruskin**

'Don't knock the weather; nine-tenths of people couldn't start a conversation if it didn't change once in a while.' **Kin Hubbard**

Most of us have access to the Weather Channel or the Met Office website, AccuWeather.com or whatever. And these are excellent sources of reliable, scientific forecasting. But they're also quite boring and don't necessarily teach us much about what actually goes on outside, and what to look out for in the countryside.

Here are some good, reasonably reliable, old-fashioned ways of weather forecasting.

▶ *Fir cones close when the air is damp. So, collect some cones and lay them out in the garden or near to your tent when you're camping. If they close, there's moisture in the air and it's probably going to rain.*

▶ *Seaweed is an excellent, highly sensitive monitor of damp air. Pick some and hang it from a branch or fence post; damp seaweed means it is likely to rain, dry seaweed anticipates dry weather.*

▶ 'Red sky at night, shepherds' delight. Red sky at morning, shepherds take warning'. If you see a red sky in the west as the sun is setting, it generally signifies a high pressure that creates dry air and stirs up dust particles, giving the sky an orange or red hue. Most major weather systems – and the jet stream – operate from the west towards the east, so this means that decent weather is on its way. For this reason, red sky in the morning may be down to the low angle of the east-rising sun illuminating cirrus clouds, the type that typically come in from the west, shortly before it rains (see p.36 for more on cloud types).

▶ I used to think that this was an old wives' tale, but I was wrong. If cows are lying down then it is likely to rain fairly shortly. It also seems that cows hate having the rain in their faces, so, if they are all facing in one direction, the rain will come from the other.

▶ I've been told that if rooks leave their nests at dawn and fly in a straight line, a fine day lies ahead. If, however, they take off later in the morning and follow a more erratic route, then rain is on the way.

▶ Some birds are excellent weather forecasters. Swallows always hunt high in the sky when the weather is fine and work closer to the ground if rain is on its way. You are likely to feel the change simultaneously, though, as this one is more about present rather than future conditions: the thermal activity on a fine day draws the insects that swallows hunt higher into the sky. When it rains, on the other hand, the insects – and their predators – seek the shelter of trees or buildings, typically lower to the ground.

▶ Seagulls tend to shelter as rain approaches.

▶ Ants often build steep-sided hills just before a storm for protection. Apparently they can sense a change in air pressure.

▶ Teach yourself a bit about clouds (see p.36). Then lie on your back, look up and, hey presto, you'll understand what's coming.

▶ Breathe deep; smell the air. Everything smells a bit stronger when there's damp in the air and rain on the way.

NAVIGATION SKILLS

'Man cannot walk in a straight line or otherwise maintain a directional course without relying on some tangible clue wholly apart from his own instincts.' **Calvin Rutstrum**

~ How to not get lost ~

If you are walking in the hills or through large woods, there's a chance that you might get lost. It has happened to me once or twice – most recently about five years ago, when a rainy Scottish day turned into a very foggy one – and it happened to one of our daughters, when she was 11 and a sunny day suddenly threw a blizzard at her. The latter one was very scary indeed for all of us; she was helped by some other walkers who had the right gear and a mobile phone.

If you're intrepid you will get lost at some point; maybe not too badly lost, but it can be frightening, none the less.

Beyond staying at home, the five best ways not to get lost are:

Carry a compass

Figure out how to use it before you head out and then make sure you understand your direction of travel before you set off. More about this below.

Use a map

Plan your route and keep an eye on the map as you progress. Be aware that the land can look amazingly different in reality to how it looks on the map if you haven't checked your location for an hour or two.

Make mental markers

If you are planning on returning the way you came, keep an eye out for landmarks such as trees, rocks, recognisable gates and fence posts as you walk. It is also a good idea to try to associate these landmarks with one another as you go. If you're lost in conversation or thought, it's easy to miss important markers.

Stick to paths

There's a logic to this (beyond not upsetting land managers and ground-nesting birds).

Plan carefully

You want to do this to make sure you are at your finishing point long before dark.

Finally, always tell someone where you are going and when you intend to return. If you have driven to a point from which to start your walk, leave a visible note in your car, saying where you are intending to go and roughly when you intend to be back, even if you are planning to camp for a couple of days.

~ What to do if you do get lost ~

Don't call Mountain Rescue

unless you consider your situation to be an emergency. Mountain Rescue is reached through the police via the standard emergency number. Assuming you are in mobile phone reception zone, though, it might be a good idea to call a friend and say that you are a bit muddled so that – if the worst comes to the worst, which it

probably won't – someone will be able to put a trace on where you are.

Stay calm

Don't panic. Sit down, have something to eat or drink and look around you. See if you can recognise any landmarks that you have passed, or are expecting to pass. Assume the position and make yourself as comfortable as possible.

Use your map

But be careful; if you're lost, wishful thinking can be dangerous. Be certain that what you see on the map is what you see on the landscape.

Remember that all rivers flow downhill

Following a river will generally lead to safety eventually. However, remember that crossing rivers, particularly those that are fast flowing, deep or in spate can be much more difficult than you might at first imagine. So, stay on the bank and follow the river instead. Eventually – in the British Isles at least – you'll reach civilisation.

Know when you need help

If you are convinced that you are lost, call the emergency services and then stay put. If you cannot make a call, the best thing is still to stay where you are.

Make some noise

Don't be embarrassed to shout or wave or draw attention to yourself. A small fire is good, too; smoke during the day, flames at night. A whistle is useful, as is a flag made from a spare jumper or jacket.

Leave a trail

If you do decide to move, imagine yourself as part of the rescue operation. Leave clues, the more obvious the better. A note of your name, the date and maybe your phone number is useful.

Listen up

If you hear an unusual noise (say a prolonged car horn or maybe a whistle) walk towards it. The chances are that this is someone looking for you.

~ Carrying the right kit ~

Good kit helps you to avoid getting lost, or in trouble and can be a lifesaver if you do get lost. You really don't have to wear nerdy, hi-performance stuff; you just need to be sensible.

Remember that it is often much colder in the hills than you could imagine. Always carry a spare jumper and some simple form of rain protection. A hat can be a godsend, too.

Never wear jeans to go walking; wet jeans are unbelievably awkward to move in. Avoid shorts if you are going for a proper long hike.

Wear a good pair of boots or trainers (see 'the best kit for the outdoors', p.243 for our favourite boots).

Carry a compass, a fully charged phone, something to eat (chocolate, Kendal Mint Cake, glucose tablets ... that sort of thing), plenty of water or high energy drinks, a map, a pen, some paper and maybe a few sandwich bags to keep things dry.

As to first aid, we like to keep this fairly simple; a couple of sticking plasters, some paracetamol and some blister plasters. We always carry blister plasters on walks or to festivals and they are invariably used.

~ Using a compass for simple directions ~

Everyone loves a compass. Every small boy has a compass. But very few people seem to know how to use one.

There are some excellent compass apps for mobile phones. But nothing beats the real thing.

A mountaineering or orienteering compass is the most common type; one that has the four cardinal points (north, south, east and west) marked on it as well as the intercardinals (northeast and so on) and the secondary intercardinals (north-northeast, etc.).

On these compasses, there is a simple red needle which always points north. There is also a direction-of-travel arrow, which is marked on the compass.

Hold your compass as steadily as possible and as level as possible, just away from your body, with the direction of travel arrow pointing towards where you're going.

Now look at the red needle; it is pointing north. As you rotate the compass, the needle stays where it is. So, if you turn the compass until, for example, the east marking is under the red part of the needle, this does not mean that the compass is pointing east. It sounds elementary, perhaps, but this is a common misapprehension. Remember: the red end of the needle always points north!

To find your direction of travel, rotate the compass until the north mark and the red part of the needle are perfectly aligned. Then you know where you are heading.

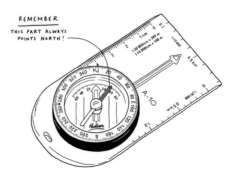

REMEMBER
THIS PART ALWAYS
POINTS NORTH!

KEEPING DOGS

~ XANTHE GLADSTONE ~

Our daughter Xanthe, who is now 16, has been animal mad all her life, and is especially mad about dogs. This is her story.

'Throughout my life we've always had pets and, as there are six of us, we've had a variety, from quails to fish to horses to guinea pigs. Always dogs, though. What makes dogs such a huge part of a family is that you always notice their presence; you're forever being hassled for attention, or having a head resting on you or seeing a tail wagging. It's nice. They give us love and happiness and in return we feed and walk them. It's a fair deal.

'It feels like something is missing when one of our dogs isn't around, or passes away. Unfortunately, our 11-year-old black Labrador recently died. Tess was a massive part of the family, mainly down to her sweet character and how attached she was to my dad and, if he ever wasn't around, me. Tess constantly wagged her tail; she was always happy and ready to be loved.

'When a much-loved family dog dies, for weeks after you find yourself still looking out for them on walks, or thinking you've missed out one to feed. This makes it sound depressing, but on average dogs will live for about 13 years, and it is worth it for all the time you have with them. You can relate your whole childhood to one dog you might have had memories with.

'I enjoy walking our dogs – in almost any weather! I always feel comfortable and relaxed when I know they are all happy, fed and exercised. It took 14 years of this to finally persuade my dad that I could look after a dog of my own. After months of trying to decide, I finally chose a whippet crossed with a Bedlington terrier. Luna is amazing! I love so much about her and, although my parents hate it, I love that I'll walk into my room and she'll be snuggled up on the end of my duvet - it's the sweetest thing.

'It is only some days that I don't feel like walking the dogs, like when it's really horrible weather outside, or if there's something I'd prefer to be doing inside, or it's last thing at night. Then, when I finally force myself outside, I don't regret it for a second. The dogs give me a sense of comfort that I can feel nowhere else in the world. I can shout anything to the dogs and they always support me; I will sing at the top of my voice on a walk, about whatever, and when I get back I feel relieved, as if half my problems have gone away. Just because the dogs were there to listen to me, and without a clue about what I was saying, they care and they love me.

'Having a fight with someone in my family is something that I absolutely hate; it's the worst feeling, especially when you are as close as we are as a family. So it's good to get outside,

with somebody who isn't involved, and have that company.

'When I was revising for my GCSEs, I took frequent breaks to walk the dogs; I often met interesting people, when they were on their own, and so was I. We'd get chatting about our dogs. They all love Luna, she's charming. Sometimes, I just say "hi" to the other dog walkers, as we check out each other's dogs, smile and walk past. Other times we chat for longer; one woman told me she thought her daughter and I would make great friends. You meet people you never would have before. It's nice to have a community like that, that brings so many different people together, just for their dogs.

'I wish everyone could respect dogs as much as we do. They are such an important part of our family. Our Labrador Comet actually talks to us, she whines all day even though she is completely happy. All the different characteristics and habits that our dogs have become so familiar to us that now we can tell when they are feeling ill or sad. It's an amazing connection to have.'

~ Things to know before getting a dog ~

▶ *Choose your breed carefully: factors to consider are size; amount of exercise; temperament; what the breed was originally bred for (to determine its characteristics and habits) and how compatible that is with your lifestyle; long hair versus short hair. Dogs, like children, need a routine and are happiest when you stick to it.*

▶ *An obedient, well-disciplined dog is a happy dog and makes your life much easier.*

▶ *Dogs are a commitment and need love and attention.*

▶ *Dogs are intelligent creatures and need to be kept busy and stimulated: a bored dog will become a destructive nuisance.*

▶ *Whatever the breed, dogs need at least one very good walk a day. Not a trip round the block on the lead, but a galloping, rough-and-tumble romp off the lead, in a park, through the fields or over the hills. Your dog will be happy but, just as important, so will you. Owning a dog means you have no choice but to get out in the great outdoors every day, come rain or shine, and breathe fresh air, feel mud or grass underfoot, enjoy the rustle of trees and, generally, escape the daily grind of whatever you're doing indoors, blow out the cobwebs, stretch your limbs, think, muse and mull.*

CLOUD IDENTIFICATION

~ CHARLIE ~

'If one always looked at the skies,
one would end up with wings.'
Gustave Flaubert

I'm not sure that there is a nicer way to pass the time on a warm, lazy day than watching the clouds.

As children, we used to lie in the grass for what seemed like hours on end, gazing up at them and marvelling at how their shapes shifted as they drifted by. And our children have done the same, as children all over the world and across the generations have done. However, unless you are a geographer, or paid particular attention in those lessons at school, the names of the common clouds may not be at your fingertips. So we asked Gavin Pretor-Pinney, founder of the Cloud Appreciation Society, to describe some of his favourite clouds, to bring the science to life . . .

CLOUD APPRECIATION

- GAVIN PRETOR-PINNEY -

'The countryside is a great place to watch clouds – there's less to distract you down on the ground than in an urban environment where you need to avoid things like being run over by a bus. In the country you can walk along in a daze, gazing up at the sky; at worst you might trip over a gorse bush or something.

'There's also, I think, a different perception of rain in the countryside. When you're wearing the right clothes – and I find I'm better prepared when I am in the country – it can even be quite enjoyable to be out in the rain. Also, observing the water cycle in an environment where everything around you depends on it, all makes a bit more sense. In the city, rain feels more of an interruption.

'The secret to spotting interesting clouds is not to go out looking for them – try too hard and you're bound only to see altostratus, "the boring cloud", which creates an overcast, featureless sky above you, rather than a beautiful cloudscape.

'Instead, be receptive, and prepared to interrupt your daily routine for a few minutes of meteorological meditation. Watching the way clouds change and mutate gradually helps us to slow down a little too. A kind of antidote to the modern world.'

~ Some of Gavin's favourite clouds ~

Clouds are categorised in the same way that plants and animals are – genus and species and, as such, the first bit has the capital letter. This may all be part of Man's futile attempts to impose an order on nature, but when you look up to see this random and wild phenomenon momentarily taking on a form we recognise, a perfect cumulonimbus, perhaps (see below), it really is a joy.

~ Altocumulus lenticularis ~

The name comes from the Latin for 'lentil'. Smooth and disc-shaped, this cloud can look very much like a UFO; you tend to see them where there are hills or mountains as they form when winds pass over the peaks, taking a wavy path. **Altocumulus lenticularis** clouds form on the crests of these wind waves, where the air rises before it tips again. Amid the wind, their position remains fixed and they hover in place.

~ Mammatus ~

Mamma is the Latin word for 'breast', and this cloud is named as it is because of its 'pouches', which hang down from underneath an overcast layer above. **Mammatus** clouds are most dramatic seen on the underside of storm clouds and, lit by a low sun, they can look almost apocalyptic. You look at them and think there's going to be the most humungous storm; they are associated with storms but generally they're at the back of storm clouds, in terms of the direction in which they tend to move. So if you see mammatus clouds, and it's not raining, it's likely that the storm has passed and you're looking at the back of it.

~ Cumulonimbus ~

This is the name of the storm clouds, mentioned above. If you're seeing them from a distance, they spread out like an anvil, or a mushroom cloud. They are enormous clouds and can extend upwards from about 600m to 12 or 16km into the sky. These clouds produce heavy showers, which tend to be relatively short-lived, as well as hail, thunder and lightning. Because they're so large, if you're underneath one all you'll be able to see is a dark and ominous brooding sky. The darker it gets, the more imminent the downpour; that's because a dark cloud base indicates that a cloud has grown very tall, and the taller a cloud, the more the sunlight above it is scattered by all the droplets and particles of ice within the cloud, rather than being able to emerge from the base.

When this storm cloud is young, it's called **Cumulonimbus calvus**, which means 'bald' in Latin. This is because the cloud starts off with a relatively smooth top. When it becomes a mature cumulonimbus, ready to produce a heavy downpour, it is called a **Cumulonimbus capillatus**, because it spreads out in high winds at its top and looks like a crazy, unruly hairstyle.

In the 1950s, a pilot in the US navy had to eject from his plane over a cumulonimbus after his engine exploded. He had an awful descent through the cloud, where his parachute opened, but – miraculously – emerged at the bottom, black and blue and swollen, to tell the tale. He'd checked his watch upon leaving the plane and again when he landed: what should have been a ten-minute descent had, in fact, taken 40 minutes. He was covered in bruises from being pummelled by hailstones and fierce turbulence inside the cloud. The differences in air pressure had caused him to swell massively, and he was bleeding from the ears from explosions of thunder. I don't know if he'd be a member of the Cloud Appreciation Society.

~ Pileus ~

To me, the pleasure of cloudspotting is in the small things that other people may miss. For this reason, **pileus**, from the Latin for 'cap', is a little cloud I really like. If conditions are right, pileus can appear momentarily on top of a **cumulus** (see below) as it grows and rises up into the atmosphere to become a storm cloud. This smooth little cloud, on top of the big, cauliflower-like cumulus, makes the latter look as if it is wearing a toupée, or maybe a Donald Trump comb-over. As the cumulus continues to grow it subsumes the pileus, giving the appearance that this toupée is falling off sideways in a rather undignified way.

~ Cumulus ~

This is the most generic cloud, and probably the one that everyone would think of if asked to name a cloud. It looks like little puffs of cotton wool and is called the 'fair weather' cloud as it forms on sunny mornings as the ground heats up and causes thermals of air to rise and expand and float up like a bubble. As it floats up, taking moisture with it, the air cools and, if it cools and rises enough, a cumulus cloud can appear. It is a light-hearted cloud and drifts along as if shepherded by the gentle breeze. You often see profiles of faces in these clouds as they have quite crisp edges compared to other clouds.

~ Cirrus ~

This high cloud – which you see around airplane-cruising altitude – is composed entirely of ice crystals. The Latin name comes from a lock of hair, as that's rather what it looks like. Or a brush of watercolour across the blue sky. I find it one of the most beautiful of the common clouds because it's so airy and translucent; it feels very free, and looking at these clouds gives you a sense of freedom too, particularly as, being so high, you see a large vista of the sky when you look at them. My daughter's middle name is Cirrus.

But none of these names are important, really. More important is how the sky makes you feel; and how seeing shapes in them feeds the imagination. You don't need to know any names of clouds or even notice there are different types; you can enjoy just seeing that one that looks like a dog ... Or one that looks like a kind of alligator . . . The very act of doing that is good for the soul; you simply can't do it when you're stressed, rushed or worried.

THE TEN MAIN CLOUD TYPES

CIRRUS

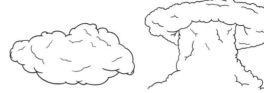

CUMULUS

CUMULONIMBUS

ALTOCUMULUS

CIRROCUMULUS

CIRROSTRATUS

ALTOSTRATUS

STRATUS

STRATOCUMULUS

NIMBOSTRATUS

~ The science bit ~

The study of clouds is a subsection of meteorology called nephology (from *nephos*, the Greek word for 'cloud') or cloud physics. Clouds have Latin names, in the same way as plants and animals do, and the cloud-naming system was created by an amateur meteorologist called Luke Howard at the start of the 19th century and formally adopted by the International Meteorological Commission in 1929.

Howard's original system established four general cloud categories based on physical appearance and how they are formed: cirriform, mainly detached and wispy, from the Latin *cirrus* (curl of hair); cumuliform, mainly detached and heaped, rolled or rippled, from the Latin *cumulus* (heap); stratiform, mainly in layers or sheets, from the Latin *stratus* (layer); and nimbus, for all clouds producing significant rain, from the Latin *nimbus* (rain).

These categories were then cross-classified into lower and upper families, so that low-level cumuliform clouds were given the genus name cumulus and low-level stratiform clouds were given the genus name stratus. Similarly, the high-level clouds were called cirrocumulus and cirrostratus respectively, and given the genus name cirrus. In the early 1840s, stratocumulus was added to the classification, describing low-level clouds mostly detached with both cirriform and stratiform characteristics, similar to upper-level cirrocumulus. Some 15 years later, altocumulus and altostratus were added, describing mid-level cloud formations, and in 1880, cumulonimbus was added to the classification, describing vertically formed clouds identifiable by their appearance and ability to produce thunder. Finally, towards the end of the 1890s, the nimbus clouds were reclassified as nimbostratus.

~ Three unusual clouds ~

~ Circumzenithal arc ~

This looks like a rainbow but is in fact a prismatic effect in very high ice clouds, when the sun is low in the sky – at an altitude of 32.2 degrees or less, to be specific.

~ Noctilucent clouds ~

These clouds are at the edge of the atmosphere and only illuminated after sunset, when the set sun's rays reflect off the clouds in the darkened sky. They have a luminous beautiful look – but are actually little understood and even possibly connected to climate change. You can only see them in parts of the world above 50 degrees north.

~ Asperatus clouds ~

These look like a rough and wavy sea viewed from beneath the waves, as though the clouds were the surface you can see from below. This is a newly categorised cloud and, in 2009, the Cloud Appreciation Society submitted the name (which means 'rough' in Latin) to the Royal Meteorological Society for formal recognition, which would make it the first new cloud-type in 60 years.

With thanks to Andrew Pothecary, friend and long-standing member of the Cloud Appreciation Society, for explaining these to us.

HOW TO TIE DIFFERENT KNOTS

~ WILLIAM GLADSTONE ~

Charlie's dad is a true countryman; he is always making things outside, or chopping things down, building things or dragging things around. He was also in the navy and – to boot – he was Chief Scout. He knows a lot about knots …

'I was a Scout during my school days from the age of 11 until I was 15, and amongst other things I learnt knots and self-reliance. Both came in useful when I left school and joined the navy, the difference being that a lot of people's safety then depended on them. About 25 years later I became Chief Scout and it was very useful when I went round Scout camps to be able to tell the boys which knot to use and, if necessary, how to make it.

'A rope gets its strength from several strands or fibres being twisted. In the old days you had to make a nice neat "whipping" at the rope end with a thin cord to stop it from unravelling. Nowadays you can just use adhesive tape. But a neater way, if it is a plastic rope (as most ropes are), is to put on a glove made from a tough material, heat the end of the rope under a candle until it turns to goo, and smooth it off with your gloved fingers.

'When a rope is not in use, make it into a coil, always working clockwise or "with the sun". Then it will uncoil easily instead of becoming a tangle. To store it, pinch the coil in the middle so it looks like a thin figure of eight, wrap one end a few times round its wasp-waist, tuck the end in so it doesn't come undone, and then it can easily be hung on a hook or just thrown down in a heap and it will be ready for use next time. This is known as hanking a rope.

'Knots get their strength from friction – either the friction of the rope itself, or the thing it is tied round. Try passing a rope once or twice round a post or a tree. Then get the youngest member of the family to hold the short end and get everybody else to try to pull the long end away. They probably won't succeed. If they do, then take three (or four) turns round the tree. If you haven't got a strong team, tie it to the car. It won't slip. (It may snap if you pull hard enough.) By the way, make sure the short end isn't too short, so the junior member doesn't get his or her fingers pinched if the trick goes wrong.

'Remember that it is just as important to be able to untie a knot as to tie it. Even if somebody's safety doesn't depend on it, you want to be able to use your rope more than once. It may be salutary to realise that even nowadays it is a cardinal rule that every yachtsman should carry a knife at all times, to cut a rope if he gets into trouble.'

~ Round turn and two half hitches ~

If the youngest member of the family is still holding that rope round the post or tree, just put a 'half hitch' knot on it. This will have exactly the same result as having the child hold on to it – as long as the half hitch doesn't come off. To prevent this, just put a second half hitch on it. (Make sure both half hitches are the same way: if they are put on in opposite ways they will jam.) You have now tied one of the most useful of all knots: a round turn and two half hitches. Congratulations! This is the best way of tying a rope to almost anything. One of its advantages is that it is very easy to get it taut if you want to. If you want to pull it tighter, take the half hitches off and ease it round the post or tree. (Then put the half hitches back on.)

~ Clove hitch ~

~ Timber hitch ~

This is a brilliantly simple knot if you want the same result as for a 'round turn and two half hitches', but with both ends of the rope taut. Start by passing a round turn round a post or a tree, and then cross the rope over itself as you start to put on a second round turn. Then simply tuck the end into the second round turn. This is just as good as a 'round turn and two half hitches' – and even simpler – except that you can't untie it while it is under tension.

There is a trick for making a 'clove hitch' very quickly and simply. Make two little loops in your rope, both in the same direction; put the second one under the first and then pop them over the end of a post.

This is the easiest of all knots. If you want to tie a rope to any post or pole or lump of wood or lump of anything in order to pull it along or raise it up, then just put the rope round it and loop the short end round the rope and twist it back round itself few times. The tension will keep it tight and in place. This is also a good way of keeping your trousers up if you have lost weight and don't have a belt or braces.

~ Reef knot ~

To tie the ends of two ropes together, cross one end over the other as if you were starting to tie up your shoes. Then do it again, but if the first cross was left lace over right lace, then the second must be right over left – or vice versa. If you do them both the same way you will not get a 'reef knot' but a 'granny' and you will be IN DISGRACE. Why? Because it won't come undone.

If you want to know why it is called a reef knot, find an ancient mariner and ask him. If he doesn't know, he has lost his marbles, so let him go and find some more. Don't let this one go, as you will need him to tell you why a sheet bend got its name, too.

In the Scouts we were taught to use a reef knot to tie the two ends of a bandage together. The reason it was so suitable for that job was that it lies nice and flat. A granny makes a lump. Nowadays sticky plaster is used instead of bandages, but a reef knot is still useful for tying two pieces of rope together.

~ Sheet bend ~

A 'sheet bend' is essential for tying two ropes of different sizes together. Take hold of the end of the thicker of the two ropes, form it into a loop and hold the point where the two bits of rope come together to make the loop between your finger and thumb. Then take the end of the thinner rope, bring it up through the loop you have formed, then right round the back of the loop and pop it back down the middle. As soon as the knot is drawn tight, it will hold.

To teach your children how to do this, first form the loop (the 'rabbit hole'), keep hold of it between your finger and thumb, and give the learner one end of the thinner rope. Tell them to bring the 'bunny' up through the hole, round the back of the tree, then back down the hole. They will come across the bunny again with the 'bowline'.

If they are too big for the bunny, tell them it's some other animal, a rat for the boys and a fox cub for the girls, perhaps.

If you want a sheet bend to hold even when it is not taut, then make the bunny go round the tree twice before going back down the hole. This is called a 'double sheet bend'.

~ Bowline ~

~ Belaying the rope ~

A bowline is used for making a loop (which won't slip) at the end of a rope. Grab a bit of rope or string and make a small loop in it about 30cm from the end. Hold the loop between your finger and thumb so that the end of the rope is above the main length of the rope. Here you have a tree with the 'rabbit hole' (see 'sheet bend') IN FRONT OF IT. Now take hold of the short end of the rope, which is the 'bunny'. Bring it up through the loop (the rabbit hole) and round behind the back of the tree (from right to left in the illustration) and then back down the hole. Gently pull it tight, and there you are! You have made your loop, which won't slip.

To 'belay' a rope means to fasten the end to something temporarily. You can tie it round a post or a tree. You can use a round turn and two half hitches, or a clove hitch plus a half hitch. But what if there is no post and no tree? You can wham in a peg with a sledgehammer, not straight but at an angle, so that the top of the peg points away from the direction of strain. If this is not strong enough, wham in a second peg behind it, or even a third, as in the illustration. This is called a picket.

If you want to tie up something like a boat regularly, then buy a cleat (a device designed for the purpose). Put the rope straight round it several times. Don't criss-cross it or put on a half hitch as it will jam under tension.

GETTING AROUND

Notes

WALKING AND WALKS

~ CHARLIE ~

'The pedestrian is the highest and most mighty of beings; he walks for pleasure, he observes but does not interfere, he is not in a hurry, he is happy in the company of his own mind, he wanders detached, wise and merry, godlike.'
Tom Hodgkinson

Walking gets a bad rap. Somewhere along the way the word 'rambler' became as much an insult as a description of someone who enjoyed wandering around in the countryside. It's a shame, because walking is one of life's great pleasures; it's free, and it doesn't really require any special kit except a pair of good boots or trainers and a jacket. And it makes you feel good about life and heals pain; but more of that later.

My parents were very bossy when it came to walking. Whenever they sensed that one of their children might be even vaguely bored they'd holler: 'Right, let's go for a walk.' Sometimes I resented this and refused to budge; but generally I'd be up and out within minutes. We walked for miles and miles as a family; the weather had no bearing on where we went or how long we stayed outside. We climbed hills and crossed rivers and walked down some of Britain's longest beaches. And it was always brilliant.

From these walks I learnt that a good yomp is better for the soul than almost anything else. Beyond the obvious benefits for your health, a good walk heals headaches or hangovers and puts pay to angst; and, of course, it gives you an appetite.

Nowadays, we walk less often than we'd like. The pressures of work and family life have pegged back the amount of time spent in the hills. But we still walk a great deal and we have tried (and generally succeeded) to teach our children the joys of a good walk.

And we have formed our own mini walking club, too. This is a loose group of friends who love walking and who egg each other on to take time off and walk and talk. Sometimes we go for a few hours. We might head to the Ridgeway for a summer afternoon if we're in London (Britain's most ancient path, stretching for 87 miles through Buckinghamshire) or we head to Wales or into the Highlands for a few days. One of the secrets of making this work is to make sure that there is a good, comfortable reward at the end of the day; a great pub, tea and cakes, fish and chips, or a hotel with a proper bath.

~ Make the most of your walk ~

Much has been written about walking etiquette, about shutting gates and picking up litter and all of that stuff. And so we won't dwell on that. Instead, here are our top tips for happy walking.

Take the flak

If you want to get a large number of adults and children outside, be prepared to be bossy/accused of being hearty. You will have to force some of the gang outside; but no one (usually) ever regrets going on a walk.

Keep small people happy

If small children are warm and dry they will be able to walk for miles. Sweets or chocolate help too. We have lured our children on some amazingly long walks by, effectively, laying a trail of treats.

Adults need treats, too

One member of our walking club always takes a flask of whisky and some Werther's Orginals with her; another takes mini pork pies and red wine.

Look after your feet
A good pair of worn-in walking boots or trainers is a must. Good socks are helpful too; there are some excellent socks on the market that almost eliminate the risk of blisters.

Decide on a route
But be prepared to deviate.

Let everyone find their own pace
And spread out. This way conversation will flow and new friendships will be made.

Say 'hello' to everyone you encounter
This sounds obvious but some people walk past in silence without as much as eye contact. We're all so caught up in our busy lives that perhaps it can be easy to forget – but it's good to force oneself to shake off modern habits. And it makes you feel good not to be quite so British.

Pick up any litter you find along the way
It might be annoying to think the person before you has thrown things on the ground but a lot of rubbish left by walkers is dropped by mistake. And someone has to pick it up.

If you can, go stick-free
Avoid those walking/ski pole things with spiked tips, if you are able – they aid erosion. All those little holes they create will fill with water or frost and eventually become bigger holes.

Be aware that cows hate dogs
So do not let them mix. We have a friend who ignored this advice and he and his small child were very nearly killed.

If you want to see wildlife, stand still
In our experience animals that crouch in the undergrowth as you amble past will be spooked – but if you stand still now and then, they will show themselves.

Brave all weathers
Remember, rain is every bit as beautiful as sun; it just depends how you look at it.

Reward yourselves
The best post-walk food is ham and baked potatoes. Particularly good with beer or sherry in the winter.

GREAT BRITISH WALKS

THESE BOOTS ARE
MADE FOR
WALKING...

It never ceases to amaze me how quickly the landscape in Britain can change or how varied it is. One minute you can be on wild moorland, and the next in tame arable fields. Walking is one of the best ways to experience the wealth of geographical differences that Britain has to offer.

Here are some walks that either we, or friends, have done; or ones that are high on our to-do list. However, do make sure you consult a map as the routes below simply sketched outlines designed to whet your appetite for the great outdoors.

For more information on these walks, see p.260.

~ Boasty walks ~

*These are walks that you do with your competitive nature to the fore,
not just for the pleasure of walking in the fresh air and countryside.*

- CORNWALL -

~ The Saint's Way ~
Padstow to Fowey

The Saint's Way is a one-day 28-mile hike through the wonderful Cornish countryside.

Legend has it that the pilgrims from Ireland crossed the Irish Sea and came up the River Camel as far as they could sail and then walked for about four miles across to the River Fowey where they picked up another boat and sailed down the Fowey and over to Spain to carry on the pilgrimage to Santiago de Compostela. The route changed over the centuries as both the Camel and the Fowey silted up, and the walking part grew longer and longer, resulting in today's route. This walk is both exhilarating and fascinating thanks to the historic remains, ancient footbridges, forgotten granite stiles that dot the way. Sadly there isn't a truly fantastic pub for lunch, so take a picnic and have it at Helman Tor, overlooking the whole county.

As it isn't a circular walk, you can either leave a car at one end, drive a second car to the other and then go back and collect it, or park at one end and take a taxi to the other end.

- THE GRAMPIANS -

~ The Mounth Road ~
*Mount Keen and The Firmounth and
Fungle Road's Glen Tanar, Aberdeenshire
to Glen Esk, Angus and back.*

This is a two-day circular hike that follows three of the ancient drove roads and trading routes in the Grampians, and takes in Mount Keen, the most easterly Munro. The route is well marked, and the going is steady, and if actually climbing the Munro isn't for you, there is a path that takes you over its shoulder. On a clear day, the views are spectacular, and you can see all the way to the sea in one direction, and the Cairngorms in the other. You can camp if you are intrepid, or there is a B&B, The House of Mark, in Invermark, Angus to break your journey. I stayed here when I did the walk in 2002, and the welcome was very warm and hospitable, and the beds comfortable.

~ Hadrian's Wall Path ~
Wallsend to Bowness-on-Solway

Hadrian's Wall is one of Britain's best-known historical landmarks and as such, surely deserves a bit of exploration. It is definitely on my 'walks to do before I get too old' list, together with John o'Groats to Land's End, and following the Thames from source to estuary.

Hadrian's Wall Path stretches for 84 miles from Wallsend on the east coast to Bowness-on-Solway on the west coast, and runs alongside the Roman fortification which, when first built by its eponymous emperor in AD 122, was around 4.5m high. The walk is obviously not something to be undertaken in one day and you can easily choose one section or another to tailor-make your ideal walk.

The walking is not difficult, and there are several companies that will help you plan an itinerary that suits you. Some will move your luggage from one B&B or campsite to the next, meaning that you need only take with you what you need for that day. The highest

and wildest part of the path runs between Chollerford and Walton, and it is from here that you get the best view of the Wall, including several important Roman forts.

~ The Ridgeway ~

The Ridgeway Path follows an ancient chalk road used by soldiers, shepherds, and travellers. It stretches for some 87 miles from Ivinghoe Beacon, north of Tring in Hertfordshire through the Chilterns, over the Thames and through the North Wessex Downs to Overton Hill. The walking is not very difficult, and the countryside and villages are very scenic. And while you can embark on the whole 87 miles, staying in pubs along the way, it is also very easy to do sections of it. Charlie and his friend Freddie walked two sections of the Ridgeway on a walking and talking weekend in 2011. They stayed at a nice pub called the Boar's Head in Ardington, near Wantage. From there it is a 30-minute walk to the Ridgeway and they walked east one day and west the next, returning to the pub for the night.

~ Sensible walks ~

These are walks that may take only a couple of hours, but are every bit as worth the effort of pulling on the walking boots as the boasty walks are.

~ DERBYSHIRE ~

~ Dovedale, Ormaston and Alstonefield ~

The Peak District in Derbyshire is a gloriously beautiful place to walk at any time of year, and many of the walks that you can follow are steeped in local or national history. We have a great friend who lives in Derbyshire and has suggested three excellent walks that he regularly does and loves. All three are circular routes.

~ Dovedale ~

The landscape here is amazing with spectacular views over the rocky hills and the River Dove, well known for its ancient stepping stones. The closing scene of the 2010 *Robin Hood* film, with Russell Crowe, was shot in an area called Thorpe Pastures which stretches down to the Stepping Stones.

~ Ormaston ~

This a lovely walk, and relatively easy-going, unless it has been raining hard. The only problem is that on a sunny Sunday in summer, the path can be quite busy.

~ Alstonefield ~

Some of the route on this 4.5-mile walk is quite steep, and can get a bit muddy, but the reward of lunch at The George in the village is a more than worthy pay-off for your hard work.

~ KINCARDINESHIRE ~

~ Clachnaben ~

Clachnaben is the granite tor that sits perched on top of the little mountain behind our house in Scotland. Legend has it that the Devil took a bite out of the hillside and found it so unpalatable that he spat it out on top of the mountain, so the small valley at the bottom of the little mountain is locally referred to as The Devil's Bite.

The walk takes a couple of hours, and the going is very easy for the first half, but then gets gradually steeper and steeper as you near the top. The path is very well maintained by a local trust, which raised a considerable amount of money to pave some of the path that was being very badly eroded by weather, walking sticks and mountain bikes. The views from the top are spectacular. The only caveat is that the weather can change dramatically very quickly. Our daughter Xanthe and her friend Georgie set off up Clachnaben with a picnic about five years ago, and by the time they got to the top, the warm spring day that they had set off in had changed to a snowstorm.

- CORNWALL -

~ Port Isaac to Port Quin ~

There are two options for this walk, you can either follow the coastal path, which our friend Harry describes as gorgeous but tough, or the gentler and easier inland route. Or you can combine the two, making it a circular route. If you strike out from Port Isaac along the coastal path, you will be faced with 200 steep steps, and that is only the first challenge. But although the route is 'severe', the views over the sweeping Cornish coastline and the invigorating sea breeze are fitting compensation for your efforts. There are plenty of great pubs in Port Isaac - if you can, wait till you have completed the circuit for that well-earned pint, or you can buy something to have when you stop to rest at the deserted village of Port Quin.

- HEREFORDSHIRE -

~ Black Hill ~

Every May, for the Hay Festival, we go and stay with some friends who live very close to the Black Hill in Herefordshire, made famous by Bruce Chatwin's novel of (nearly) the same name. More often than not, we find time to squeeze in a walk, and here are two of the best, appropriately with a literary twist.

~ The Cat's Back ~

The Cat's Back, so called because it looks like a cat waiting to pounce if you look at it from the

Herefordshire side, is the spur that leads up to Black Hill. From the top, you look over the Olchon Valley, below Offa's Dyke. It is a glorious, circular walk, and isn't that hard, especially if you have the lure of lunch at The Bull's Head in Craswall at the end of it. Park in the Black Hill car park and walk from there. Owen Sheers' wonderful novel *Resistance* is set here.

~ Hay Bluff to Hatterall Hill along Offa's Dyke ~

This walk marks the Herefordshire/ Wales border. It is a longer walk, about nine miles, but although this is a one I personally haven't done, the lunch stop at Llanthony Priory, just below the ridge in Llanthony Valley is, we've been told, more than adequate recompense for the energy expended and the views are fabulous.

~ Wormwood Scrubs ~

I am always amazed at how it feels I'm out in the great outdoors when I am walking the dogs on the very urban Wormwood Scrubs. For anyone who doesn't know them, or it, the Scrubs is an area of land owned by Hammersmith and Fulham Council in the west of London. Made infamous by the proximity of the prison and the fact that for a long time it was a wild area of heathland populated by gangs and drug lords, it is now a local nature reserve and is a joy to walk on. You meet all manner of people there: cheery dog owners, committed runners, out in all weathers, an old chap who has a gypsy pony and trap that he trots around the outer path, and at weekends, the designated football pitches are well used by local teams, and the model aircraft area is buzzing with activity. The cavalry practises manoeuvres for big displays, and there is a little area where meadow pipits are left in peace to breed. And you can barely hear the roar of London traffic.

~ North Antrim Coast ~

I am told reliably by a great friend, Emily, that one of the most spectacular walks in Northern Ireland is the Giant's Causeway and along the cliffs of the North Antrim Coast. Even though she and her family have been there hundreds of times, it still never fails to impress, and they always take friends there when they come to stay. The Giant's Causeway is a site composed of 40,000 regular-shaped basalt columns packed closely together. They were formed by the cooling and shrinking of molten lava over 60 million years ago. Although the stones are a huge tourist attraction, most people never venture beyond these. However, if you do go beyond this point (which Emily always does) there is a wonderful walk at sea level and then you climb 162 steep steps up to the cliffs above. From here you have amazing views across to the Scottish Isles on a clear day.

It is a circular walk and takes around an hour and a half and is about two miles long. There is a car park at the visitors centre, which is owned by the National Trust and so you will have to pay to park your car unless you are an NT member.

At the entrance to the car park there is an old Victorian schoolhouse that has been converted into a pub called The Nook. It is a great pit stop at the end of the walk for a pint of Guinness and they do good fresh fish and chips, seafood chowder, Irish stew and other traditional food. They often have live Irish music playing and there are open turf fires.

The nearest town is Bushmills, which makes the finest Irish malt whiskey in Ireland. Here you can visit Ireland's oldest licensed whiskey distillery, although no one under the age of eight is allowed!

And if you want a real adrenaline rush, then drive ten minutes further on from the Giant's Causeway, following the signposts to Carrick-a-Rede. This is a somewhat terrifying rope bridge that is part of a two-mile circular walk, but great fun if that's your thing.

RIDING

'A horse is dangerous at both ends and uncomfortable in the middle.' **Ian Fleming**

'A horse is the projection of peoples' dreams about themselves – strong, powerful, beautiful – and it has the capability of giving us escape from our mundane existence.' **Pam Brown**

Riding, or horseback riding as it is sometimes referred to, gets bad press. It is often seen as a somewhat elitist activity that only very horsey types take part in. It is a shame that riding has this reputation, because it isn't necessarily the case.

Even if you don't have access to a horse or live in a city, or have little or no experience, there are plenty of opportunities to get out there and enjoy the great outdoors on horseback.

In my experience, the riding community falls into two distinct categories, those who love riding for the joy of being outdoors, on horseback, for the freedom that it brings, and those who love riding for the competitive element, whether it be showjumping, dressage, cross-country, hunting or showing. Within this category, there is a subsection, the Pony Club Mothers, who love the competitive element for themselves and their children. Think Thelwell cartoons. I spent much of my childhood and early teens in the competitive category, but I now fall very definitely into the first category.

Riding holidays really are, I think, the best way of getting to enjoy riding in the great outdoors. You can of course find a riding stables close by, and go for an hour's hack, but that just isn't the same as being in the saddle for three or four hours, getting to know your horse, chatting to your companions and seeing landscape that can take your breath away. Of course, riding schools are an excellent place to start if you need to learn or relearn the basics and get a bit of practice in. For the real deal, you need to take a leap of faith and get out there.

I've explored the wilds of Andalucía on horseback with a group of girlfriends, stopping for sherries mid-morning, learning to cook the region's food, being talked through the flora, fauna and the wildlife there by fascinating experts. A few of us also saved up to do the same sort of thing through the Wadi Rum desert in Jordan, which was an amazing, life-enhancing, even life-changing experience, sleeping under the stars each night, riding through astonishing landscapes during the day, learning about Lawrence of Arabia, the Berber people and the trenches that the Americans dug across the mudflats to stop Saddam Hussein landing Iraqi jets there. There's no way you could cover the amount of ground we did on foot, or get as close to certain parts even if you were in a 4 x 4.

There are also plenty of riding holidays for grown-ups in the UK and, whether here or abroad, there are companies that will do all the organising for you, some even offering trips for complete novices. So being 'horsey' isn't a prerequisite. Either way, you'll be matched with a horse according to your experience and often there's the opportunity to go out without guides or to spend the night in different places, riding during the day to get there. It's a great way of getting to know people, too. There is almost nothing better than to be able to go out for a ride, out in the countryside on the back of a horse, to get some quiet time away from the pressures of daily life, where silence, nature and the great outdoors reign. As it is much more physical than people might think, at the end of a long ride it is your body, rather than your mind, that is tired, which is a good thing. There may be a bit of leather between you and your horse, but the whole point of riding is that you control your horse through the pressure of your legs and the pressure of your hands on the reins. To do it reasonably well, you simply have to be in tune with the animal underneath you. Very quickly, you develop a relationship with the horse, learning its quirks, its idiosyncrasies.

There's also the frisson, the element of danger, which can be strangely liberating. Riding is considered to be a dangerous sport, and that makes it thrilling. However much in control you are, if you're galloping across the mudflats, you get a real adrenaline kick and even if you're not an adrenaline junkie that feels good.

~ Finding somewhere to ride ~

Finding the right riding centre can be very hit and miss, so I asked Nigel, who co-founded Ride Worldwide (and whose opinion I trust), to recommend a few riding holiday centres in this country. For information on these, along with some more details about what his company offers, see p.261.

Nigel also offered some advice about choosing places to do a riding holiday: 'When looking for the right riding centre for your needs,' he says, 'do ask lots of questions. Enquire about things such as: group sizes; whether they cater for novices; how much you're expected to carry with you on the horse; how long you'll be riding for; how often the horses go out and what sort they are; whether the place also does things such as schooling, showjumping, dressage and so on (which might give you a bit more insight into the quality of the horses – and the staff), the ratio of road-riding to off-road, and also whether you need to bring your own hat and riding boots or special clothing.'

~ Riding ~

Some dos , don'ts and misconceptions

▶ If the horse gallops off with you don't lean forward, which is the natural instinct. If you lean forward the horse will go faster, so you have to go counter to your instinct and sit up, as heavy in the saddle as you can.

▶ If you're going across tricky ground let the horse pick its way – don't try to guide it. The horse will know best.

▶ Don't feed horses mints as they're bad for their teeth. A carrot is better.

▶ Never walk behind a horse you don't know. Most horses kick because they're frightened of what's behind them, so gently let it know you're there.

▶ Horses can bite really hard. If you are offering a horse an apple or carrot, hold it in the flat of your hand. Read the signals, and if a horse has its ears flat back, it doesn't like you or something you are doing, so step away.

▶ Horses can sense if you're frightened so start with the right ride for your experience and never tell the person in charge of allocating horses that you are better than you are.

▶ You don't need the full riding kit to get started but don't wear jeans as the seams on the inside legs really rub. Tight trousers with soft seams or sturdy leggings are best if you don't have jodhpurs. On your feet, make sure you wear something with a heel, so that you don't slip out of the stirrups. Trainers are a bad idea.

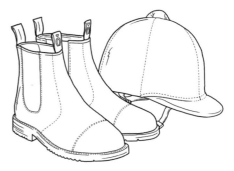

WHERE TO GO CYCLING

'The bicycle is the most civilised conveyance known to man. Other forms of transport grow daily more nightmarish. Only the bicycle remains pure in heart.'
Iris Murdoch

'When I see an adult on a bicycle, I do not despair for the future of the human race.' **HG Wells**

- WARWICKSHIRE -

~ River Avon, Warwickshire ~

Circular 15-mile route starting and finishing at the Traditional Bicycle Shop, Stratford upon Avon, via Loxley, Charlecote, Hampton Lucy, Alveston and Tiddington. Allow three hours minimum.

'We are so lucky here,' says Ian Parkes of the Traditional Cycle Shop (see p.262). 'It really is brilliant cycling country. On the third Saturday of every month myself and the chaps from the shop dress up in our tweeds and flat caps and take our traditional Pashley bicycles out on a three-hour run that's great for families, couples – or, in our case, a small group of friends. This is a lovely route, with a few stops, which makes the ride feel a little more like a day out than a straight cycle route.

'The journey takes you across the River Avon and through Loxley, a village with a wonderful old church, a proper local pub and a beautiful imposing rectory. You'll also pass Charlecote Park, home to mighty-looking stags and playful young deer, and the grounds to Charlecote House, one of the most architecturally impressive National Trust properties in the Midlands. Stop for a cuppa and a big wedge of cake at the cafe. If – as we usually do! – you eat a bit too much cake, you could take a detour through Hampton Lucy before riding back through Charlecote village following the course of the river. This stretch of the Avon is really beautiful. At Alveston village green, you might fancy a pint of Old Hooky in The Ferry. To get to it, you turn down the wonderfully named Kissing Tree Lane. From here it is just a mile back to Stratford upon Avon and the shop (though don't let it tempt you to drink too many Old Hookys).'

WHY A PASHLEY? When we sold tricycles at Pedlars we sold the only one that really counts, by Pashley. And when we were looking for a delivery bike for our London shop, we soon discovered that the best were by Pashley. We asked Ian to verify this for us.

'The bicycles, unlike many others being produced now, are still handmade in Britain, in fact here in Stratford upon Avon itself. Pashley was established in 1926 and has been building quality bicycles ever since. They maintain their original components, with Sturmey Archer gears and Brooks Leather saddles. Brooks saddles, which adorn almost all Pashleys, were first made in 1866 and designed to replace the uncomfortable excuses for seats that were being used at the time, taking inspiration from the leather saddles of the horse-riders. Brooks saddles continue to be made by hand and are more than

just a practical item. Brooks and Pashley are things of real beauty and that's why everyone should ride one at some point in their life. Not only are they practical ... they look the business!'

* To find more details of the following routes and other cycling tours, see p.262.

~ The Elan Valley, Powys ~
various routes

'There are a lot of man-made tracks for mountain biking in this part of Wales; but those are where the masses head for, and they get packed,' says Clive Powell who runs a local bike hire business. 'But those in the know come to the Elan Valley. It's out in the wild, and you can get up onto the open hills; up there you get a great sense of freedom ... the scenery is spectacular – and on sunny days you'll hear skylarks chattering. You probably won't see another bike all day.'

Clive recommends two options in this area, also known as the 'Welsh lakelands', depending on how hardy a cyclist you are. One takes you through challenging terrain up in the hills to a network of rights of ways that will confront you with rocks, steep inclines, mud and water; the other is a gentle 18-mile, there-and-back route and very flat as it runs the length of five, 100-year-old dams following the old Birmingham Corporation Railway from Cwmdauddwr and ending at Craig Goch Dam. En route there is a visitor centre that, according to Clive, 'is fairly basic but does good, home-made cake.'

'The Victorian, stone-built dams along the route are feats of architecture,' says Clive, 'and the water is soft and clear, tinged brown, because of the peat, and lovely to drink – and there are lots of fish in it for those interested in fishing.' (For permits, see p.262). There is also plenty of other wildlife, including red kites, merlin, buzzards and squirrels. 'It really is a great place to be,' says Clive.

~ The Rodings, Essex ~
25-mile circular route from Great Dunmow through The Rodings

People often think of Essex 'as some kind of extension of east London', says Tim Gunn who runs The Old Bicycle Company, near Great Dunmow. 'But around here it's very rural, there's lots of farmland and lovely countryside. It's a very unexplored part of the world.'

Tim recommends exploring The Rodings, a group of villages based around the River Roding, which has its source in Essex and flows into the Thames. Legend has it that the Vikings rowed their boats up it. If you start at Tim's shop, where you can hire a bike, you head towards Good Easter, just before which is Titus Well, a ford where, Tim says, 'you can play Pooh sticks over the bridge. And apparently fairies live in the water meadow next door . . .' His route takes in miles of gently undulating farmland, old Essex barns and manor houses, as well as the remains of a Norman castle, at Pleshey, and a traditional Essex pub, The Compasses, at Littley Green.

Tim recommends stopping here for a 'huffer', a kind of sandwich and a local speciality. In the early spring, the lanes are full of primroses and cowslips, or 'peggles' as they're locally known. In the late spring the lanes are full of cow parsley or 'cow mumble' as it's sometimes called by locals, 'mumble' because when the cows chew it 'they make a mumbley noise - or they look like they should be!' You might also see some deer and hear birdsong from sparrowhawks, blackbirds and skylarks.

To return, you retrace your steps through Pleshey and onto North End, Onslow Green and Pentlow End. Tim recommends a little detour through the school village of Felstead which 'looks a bit "Harry Potter-ish" and is very pretty'. There are a few tea shops there, too, if you need more sustenance to make it back home.

~ Loch Katrine ~
a family-friendly half-day route,
which crosses the loch by steamship

Loch Katrine was made famous by Sir Walter Scott's epic poem *The Lady of the Lake*, and Queen Victoria, who loved the area too. Byron and Shelley were also visitors here, and some of the film *The 39 Steps* was shot on Katrine. And now, rather brilliantly, you can ride a bike not only around the loch, but also – sort of – across it, on a cycle-friendly Victorian steamship.

The ride starts at Trossachs Pier in time to catch the 10 a.m. boat with your bikes. The SS *Sir Walter Scott* is a lovely 110-year-old old steamer. 'Children love it,' says Mark Shimidzu who runs local cycle hire shop, Katrine Wheelz (see p.262). It takes less than an hour to cross the loch to Stronachlachar Pier at the west end of Katrine; from there, you ride around the head of the loch and back along the north side, which takes two or three hours. There's plenty of wildlife to see: '...red squirrel, pine martens, deer, heron and possibly osprey,' says Mark. 'There are also a few picnic sites en route; Brenachoille Point is particularly nice.' And on the ride back, you'll pass Glengyle, birthplace and childhood home of Rob Roy in the late 1600s.

The cycling part is about 13 miles, and tarmac all the way, with only a few hilly bits. If you want something more demanding, you could always add an afternoon trip to Callander, through various forest paths and past two other picturesque lochs. 'Lots of people do that,' adds Mark, 'but it is another nine miles. We do have a hire centre there too, though, so at least you won't have to do it both ways – unless you want to, of course!'

~ Thames Path ~

A 30-mile one-way ride from Putney Embankment to Staines train station (bikes are allowed on London overground trains – so you won't be stranded with your wheels if you'd rather not cycle back).

Even the capital can become rural, if you pick the right part. Something that cycling instructor Graham Hills knows well. He runs Biker's Delight, which organises guided tours in various parts of the South East, from girls-only trips and weekenders, to trips up London's waterways (see p.262 for further details). Over to you Graham ...

'The Thames Path is one of the UK's National Trails. The route runs for 184 miles, from the source of the river in the Cotswolds to the Thames Flood Barrier. The majority of it is completely flat and provides contrasting views of city and countryside. Travelling from Putney to Staines takes you along the course of the Oxford and Cambridge Boat Race, past the stylish Richmond waterfront, then on to the majestic Hampton Court, where the Palace – with its famous maze – was once occupied by Henry VIII.

'After that the riverside becomes more relaxed, with sailing clubs and village cricket pitches, before you reach your destination of Staines.

'There's a farmers' market on certain days at Dukes Meadows on the other side of Hammersmith Bridge for snacks.

'Some other highlights along the route include: Kew Gardens – or at least its gates if you don't have time for a visit; Syon House, part of the Duke of Northumberland's state; the 400-year-old Ham House and Teddington Lock where the river is no longer tidal and you can watch boats working their way through the gates. Stop for lunch at one of the riverside pubs in Walton-on-Thames, and either stay south and take a fun trip across on the Shepperton ferry, or go north over Walton bridge, leaving the river as there are stiles on the footpath that prevent cycling. When you pick up the river again at Chertsey bridge you're nearly at Staines town centre and the train station. Where you can give your weary legs a rest!'

A friend of a friend, Michael, has done quite a bit of cycling in Northern Ireland. Here are his tips for where to go with your wheels . . .

~ The Mournes ~
Newcastle, Dundrum and Tollymore Forest, County Down

'The Mourne mountains are great for walking as well as cycling. Start at Newcastle, the ideal base with its nice cafes, the beach and bike hire, and take a circular loop via the pretty Tollymore Forest Park. A marked, traffic-free route leads you out of the town and up towards the fir trees on the Mournes, where there are great views across the Irish Sea. Then it is largely flat and downhill through the park, where there is a Portakabin cafe for refreshments. Leave the park through the main entrance and then it's just a quick spin downhill on the road back.

'A less steep route via Dundrum means you could stop to eat at the Dundrum Inn (*Dundruminn.co.uk*). This is also close to the Murlough National Nature Reserve, which is surrounded by a stunning estuary, as well as heathland and forest.

Once across the estuary, you are on the road towards the fantastic Tyrella beach. Heading back from here towards Newcastle, you get great views back across Dundrum Bay, where (as the song goes) "the mountains of Mourne sweep down to the sea".'

~ Downpatrick and Strangford Lough ~

'This peninsula on the east coast is really lovely and gently undulating; part of the riding is also on the edge of Strangford Lough, an Area of Outstanding Natural Beauty, rich with wildlife and studded with little islands. There are also lovely villages en route – especially the ferry port of Strangford itself, on the seaside of the peninsula; the Lough is famous for its seafood, particularly its oysters, so make sure you taste some while you're there.

'Across the Lough, and also lovely, is Portaferry with its multicoloured cottages. Ideally plot a route that takes in the 20-minute ferry ride across the Lough (you can take your bike on board). If you're lucky, you might even see some seals.

'The best route taking in the ferry would be to start in Downpatrick, where the ancient cathedral's history dates back to 753. As for more recent history, the members of the band Ash are all from here, and went to Downpatrick High. The ferry goes from Strangford: on the other side of the water, do a loop to include Cloughey Beach with its golden sands and clear waters. Alternatively, stay on the Strangford side and do the Van Morrison trail: the Northern Irish singer's "Coney Island" refers to the headland, here, between Killough and Ardglass, where Morrison describes stopping ". . . for a couple of jars of/Mussels and some potted herrings in case/We get famished before dinner".

Michael's other tips for Northern Irish cycling . . .

~ The Sperrins ~

These hills, the birthplace of Seamus Heaney, are near the western border with the Republic of Ireland and are another Area of Outstanding Natural Beauty. Though hilly, there are routes through wooded glens, ancient villages – and welcoming pubs! – to suit many abilities.

~ The Fermanagh lakes ~

Cycle around the lakes at Enniskillen, where a ferryman will take you and your bike across the water. You can also explore steep clifftops, magical caves and well-tended wetlands, parks and forests. There is a good (though very long) Sustrans route that you could easily choose to do a section of.

~ The Antrim coast ~

On the Costal Causeway route you could, technically, go from Londonderry to Belfast, but there is a manageable 20-odd-mile route that takes in the Giant's Causeway and the summer-only 24m rope bridge (which you may, age depending, remember from a Guinness advert in the 1980s). Crossing it is an exhilarating experience – unless you suffer from vertigo. (See also p.61, on walking, for more on this route.)

LIVESTOCK

Notes

KEEPING BEES

~ PAMELA BRICE ~

Pamela Brice is Pedlars public relations manager at the Glen Dye HQ in Kincardineshire, Scotland. But when she's not manning the phones or liaising with the press, she's tending to her beehives ...

'**I first got a hankering for beekeeping in Africa** as a teenager. A local guide, while I was travelling in Botswana, pointed out a small bird called the Honeyguide - which does exactly what it says. The bird led us to a hollowed-out tree, and inside there was the buzzing mass of a bee colony. Mr Fish, the guide, lit a fire in the tree's base - smoke calms honeybees - then stuck his bare hands into the hollow and brought out dripping combs of honey, which we ate on the spot. It was delicious, and so inspiring; I'm certain this is where my passion stems from.

'**You couldn't be much more in touch with nature.** You're right in there with it all, watching at close quarters.

'**My bees are definitely the boss.** You can't dictate when they will start making honey; you're simply following these amazing insects through their life cycle. In spring, for example, I love seeing them go off to the gorse and broom to collect pollen; they come back to the hive covered in it, literally fluorescent orange. In winter, when the flowers stop producing pollen, they hunker down in the hive, forming a great mass to keep each other warm and feeding on the honey they've collected over the summer months.

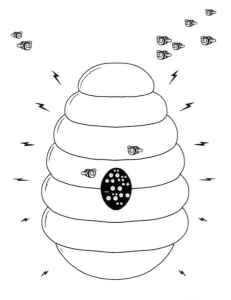

'**Beekeeping is a fascinating and gratifying hobby.** There's constantly so much to learn.

'**One hive has about 60,000 bees in it.** If they all decided you were bad news you'd be in trouble, so you have to respect them. I've been badly stung before - it was a healthy reminder that you're dealing with something that could, in a worst-case scenario, kill you.

'**I get about 28 jars of honey from one hive** after a good summer. I take a jar over to people's homes for dinner instead of a bottle of wine.

'**It's not just about honey.** I also make beeswax and use it as a furniture polish. And my son is a keen drummer and uses it to wax his drum. You can also make candles.

'**I feel a real affinity towards my bees, I'm very fond of them.** They're not pets, of course, and occasionally you accidentally squash one. You can't start shedding tears over that. But if I lost a whole colony I'd be very upset.'

Interested in keeping bees?
Pamela shares some
beginners' tips …

▶ Do your research: make sure you know what you're taking on and that you have somewhere to put a hive. I'd wanted to put mine close to the house but my husband wasn't happy. If you have neighbours run it by them – and check they don't have allergies to bee stings.

▶ Join your local club where you can learn lots and borrow equipment; particularly good for things like a honey extractor, which is big and expensive and something you only need once a year.

▶ You'll need to buy the essentials, of course, including your hive. There are mail-order websites that sell you all you'll need – even your bees. Have a look at thorne.co.uk, based in Edinburgh, for starters – they deliver nationwide. Queen bees can be posted but swarms need to be collected, so find a local supplier.

▶ Bees can cope with fairly extreme cold but cannot deal with water in the hive. So, make sure that yours is waterproof (but also well-ventilated).

▶ Bees thrive in urban environments too, and you can keep a hive on a rooftop garden, on an allotment or in your garden. You might want to check with neighbours first though.

▶ The end of the season, when the flowers have stopped producing pollen, is the time to go into the hives and take your share of the honey. The bees, understandably, get pretty angry so cover up well and think the process through: have everything you need to hand – including a smoker, fired up and ready. You want to be in and out quickly and efficiently.

▶ To make beeswax: once you've extracted the honey from the comb, you melt it down in a bain-marie and pour it into a mould sifting out any impurities; a sturdy yoghurt pot or something, anything that can withstand hot wax.

▶ There are very few wild bees around these days, so you can't, typically, just happen upon a swarm to catch. So you'll probably need to buy your first colony. The next you should be able to catch yourself, because a colony often swarms during the summer, which is when they are catch-able (see below

for more on that). In Scotland the season for it is late June, early July.

▶ The old queen bee leaves the hive, along with around half of the bees, they send out a few scouts to find a suitable new home. The rest of the swarm cluster around the queen, creating a big ball of bees – just like the ones that form 'bee beards'. They might hang from the branch of a tree or mass under a bush for anything between two hours and two days, waiting for the scouts to return. That's the moment to catch them, because they're all together. You'll need protective clothing, and a swarm catching bag on a pole, with a drawstring to close it once the bees are inside. Then you tip them onto the step of the new hive at last light and just watch them walk in – and, if they like their new home, they'll stay and you're all set.

▶ Meanwhile, in your original hive, with a new queen on the throne laying eggs to build up the population again, the bees are starting the cycle all over again ...

KEEPING HENS

~ MIRANDA McHARDY ~

There is nothing quite like a nest-warm fresh hen's egg, soft-boiled with Marmite soldiers, for breakfast. And you might be surprised at what a joy keeping hens is. We have three very old, much-loved hens who still valiantly lay an egg each a day during the spring, summer and autumn. I know that winter is definitely on its chilly way when the hens stop laying. We love our hens, but our friend and neighbour, Miranda, is a true enthusiast, and these are her words about keeping hens:

'The first thing anyone should remember about hens, is never to call them chickens. A chicken is something that you take out of the oven for Sunday lunch. A hen is a gorgeous bosomy mass of fluffy feathers that struts about the garden in a purposeful way with a beady eye out for grubs and worms.

'The eggs you get from keeping hens are the best you will ever taste. I never tire of seeing a new egg sitting invitingly on the straw in the nesting box; perfectly shaped, sometimes warm and smooth dark brown or even blue, if you are lucky and have the right hens.

'Hens give me more than eggs, they cheer me up on the grimmest of days, and if I get the chance I love to sit in the vegetable garden watching them go about their hen business, clucking to each other quietly as they scratch the ground, then quickly stepping back to have a good look to see what they have unearthed. Or dusting themselves industriously under the raspberries. Every day when I go to feed my hens, they all come running; if you have never seen a hen running towards you, head down, wings tucked up and sticking out to the sides, legs going like the clappers, you are missing one of life's simple pleasures. It will bring a smile no matter how bad the day is looking. And when I shut them up at night, they are all cosy on their perch, side by side, and their crooning conversation has almost come to an end as they go to sleep.

'My hens all have names: Samantha is the boss and the biggest; she's a Maran hen. Marans have dark-slate grey feathers, they are large hens and lay the most beautiful dark brown eggs. Netty is a Light Sussex crossed with Buff Orpington; she is blonde, lays pale-brown eggs and has the fluffiest knickers you have ever seen. Rod and Stewart are both Cream Legbars, beautiful brown speckledy hens, and they lay the prettiest little blue eggs.

'Hens are much pickier about food than legend would have it, in my opinion: they do not like any old scraps; they love cooked potatoes and, if you can face boiling up the skins, these are particularly popular. Don't feed them raw vegetables, as they will turn up their beaks and give you a dirty look. A big favourite is spaghetti and so I always make sure I cook extra now. The sight of eight hens arguing over a bit of spaghetti is worth seeing. The other thing they adore is mozzarella, and they'll do anything to get at that before the others see it. I am quite sure that hens are not supposed to have these supplements to their diet – and most of the time they get organic layers pellets, and grain. But what is life if you can't have the odd treat?

'Hens get bugs, like dogs get fleas. Once I noticed that April was looking a bit uncomfortable in her nether regions; she kept sitting down to rest on her way across the garden. I picked her up and, as advised by an expert, laid her on her back on my lap ("A hen will lie doggo if you put it on its back," apparently). She sort of did, but not for long. All the feathers on her underside were caked in what looked like grey dust. Her skin was inflamed and red and the feathers were falling out. I popped her in a picnic basket and headed for the vet. She had northern mite: each grain of 'dust' was, in fact, an egg which would hatch and then suck the blood. Untreated, she would end up anaemic and eventually die. "All you have to do," explained the vet as she handed me a bottle of dog anti-flea shampoo, "is give her a bath." Cue a huge intake of breath: what a relief.

'Back home, I got hold of her and, with one hand holding her down, applied the flea shampoo to all the infected feathers. After rubbing it in I poured the warm water over her to rinse off all the grey that,

much to my surprise, washed off easily. I was left with a very soggy-looking but clean hen who glared at me as she tried to assemble some kind of dignity back in the picnic basket. When I let her go in the garden to dry off I thought her feathers would never recover; she looked awful, but after a day or two in the sunshine she was back to her magnificent self. I had to spray the henhouse with insecticide, and give all the other hens a bath too ... but that is another story!'

Now for some hen facts and figures:

▶ *You do not need to keep a cockerel. A lot of people think that hens only lay eggs if they're 'being seen to' by a cockerel, but this is not the case. A cockerel will fertilise eggs if you want chicks, but your hens will still lay eggs without one. And you will sleep better.*

▶ *The Serama is the smallest breed and the largest is the Jersey Giant.*

▶ *Hens can live up to ten years – so make sure you're in for the long haul.*

HOME
SWEET
HOME

▶ Your henhouse needs to be weatherproof and protected against predators. Ideally it should be raised off the ground to stop rats moving in underneath. If it is a full metre off the ground it provides shelter from the rain and sun, and keeps the ground dry enough for good dust baths (as well as thoroughly enjoying a good roll around, this is how hens keep lice at bay, and keep their skin in good condition).

▶ Good ventilation is also important. Nesting boxes need to be low down and in the darkest corner for your hens to be able to lay happily. And you need to allow a minimum of a one square foot of space per hen.

▶ A 6m square run would be big enough for four hens. A fully enclosed fox-proof and bird-of-prey-proof run is best, although electric poultry-fencing can be good too. Never underestimate how clever predators are . . .

▶ A good supply of fresh water is vital for a hen's well-being.

▶ Urban dwellers need not miss out on the joys of keeping hens. There are very state of the art hen houses like the Omlet or Eggloo which are suitable for small gardens, but hens do make a mess . . . and for the sake of neighbourly peace, cockerels are definitely out of the question.

▶ Good breeds for laying are hybrids like Blackrocks or Hylines as they rarely 'go broody', in other words, these breeds are not prone to sitting on their eggs and incubating them, trying to make them hatch. Other popular breeds are the Light Sussex, the Rhode Island Red and the Orpington, which can all become very tame and are great with children. Legbars and Araucanas lay gorgeous blue eggs, and the ever-popular Maran lays wonderful dark-brown eggs.

▶ Double-yolked eggs (thought, by some, to be a sign of good luck) are very rare, about one in 1,000, so you are very lucky if you get one. The record number of yolks found in one egg is nine.

STUFF TO DO

Notes

OUTDOOR GAMES

~ CHARLIE ~

We have six children and they often have lots of friends to stay. And sometimes a bit of organised activity is necessary. So, we herd the children outdoors and get some sort of game going.

The key thing with big group games is to make them challenging and anarchic enough for the older children and, simultaneously, fun and engaging for the small ones. This doesn't always work, but more often than not it does – and our massive free-for-all games have become somewhat legendary in our (admittedly small) circle of friends.

An adult may have to be quite bossy to get people going the first time you play these; but we promise it'll be easier thereafter.

Some of these games are traditional – but, as you'll see, we've given them our own twist.

~ Volleyball ~

This is definitely our most popular family game. We have played several hundred games over the last decade and one summer some of the children's friends even had team T-shirts made for everyone. We have played with up to 25 people and it is chaotic and brilliant fun. You'll need a decent net – we got ours on Amazon; make sure it is a good, big one and not a rubbish, tiny version. And like all sports, it takes a few games to raise the standard to a challenging level (vital if you want to engage the more sporty among your gang).

We're not entirely sure of the detailed rules – it's broadly based around five games with the aim of getting a maximum of 21 points to win each one, and clear guidelines for what constitutes 'out'. But you can just decide on your own rules. Our version goes like this.

Split the players into two teams by age, sex (girls versus boys always ends in a row, because the boys are generally considered too aggressive) and ability. Make sure it is clear to older children that the little ones need to have fun, too (we let anyone who can't serve just chuck the ball when it comes to their turn; this is often enough to make the smaller players feel involved).

The ball can be passed between teammates on the same side of the net several times: make a decision about how many touches (i.e., hits of the ball) a team can have, by how many members there are on each side; if there are half a dozen, three touches will do, but if there are 12 per side then six touches is about right.

Players can touch the ball with any part of their body, so kicking, chesting or heading is fine. And they can touch it twice (or more), provided that they do so with different body parts; using two different hands does not count. Our garden has a steep slope so, to keep things fair, we change ends when one side reaches halfway to the winning score.

~ Massive bulldogs ~

ME?

We weren't sure what to call this game; it doesn't really have a name. But it is a variation on British Bulldog (kind of a cross between sprinting and wrestling in case it wasn't part of your playground experience - and itself good fun provided it is not played violently). Our version is always hugely popular and its ultimate accolade was when one 12-year-old guest described the day we introduced it to him it as 'the best day of my year'. Play it on a large scale and it can last all afternoon.

In a nutshell, the game involves two teams - the Escapees and the Guards - and the object is for the Escapees to get back to a specified starting point - within an allotted timeframe - without being spotted by the Guards. If they are caught by the Guards, they must defect to their team. There should only

be two or three Guards to start with but there can be as many Escapees as want to play. If the Guards manage to absorb every Escapee into their team, they will win - though, strictly speaking, it's not about winning or losing - it's much more about having fun while playing it.

First, you'll need to select a large area of woodland. In Scotland this is fine, due to the access laws. Elsewhere it may be less legal; so make your own mind up. We also play it in France and, although we're not exactly sure what the law is, we have never been challenged for playing in the woods and are fairly sure we're not causing any harm. This is an exciting game and the more scrambling and jumping and diving, the better. So, choose your location with this in mind.

Once you've picked your spot, select a point to which the Escapees must return - and a time before which they should aim to do it - and then drive them to a starting point as far away as you dare. The first time you play, it's probably best to limit it to a couple of miles. (Now you see why you need so much woodland.) The Guards should roam around the woods trying to spot escapees – they can split up to do this, but not too much as teams should stay close together so that no one gets lost.

Next, lay down some basic rules:

All of the Escapees must stick together – say within a 100m of one another – and go as slowly as the slowest member of their team.

No phones should be used, other than in an emergency (and no cheating!).

The Guards cannot go within several hundred metres of the starting/ finishing points.

If a Guard does spot an Escapee, then they have to identify them by name (a good tip is for the Escapees to swap clothes; it makes them harder to identify). If successfully spotted, the Escapee must join the Guards. The Guards then have to close their eyes and give the remaining members of the opposition two or three minutes to get out of sight. If some of the Escapees make it back to base within the chosen time, that team wins – though, as already said, winning isn't strictly the aim – so, really, simply making it back within the allotted time counts as achieving the game's goal.

~ Extreme croquet ~

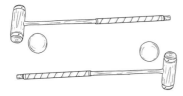

Croquet gets a bad rap. It has a reputation for being snooty, boring and over-refined – probably because it's something you tend only to see being played in period dramas. But our version is aggressive, frustrating and great for all ages. And don't take our word for it – we know of at least five children who have forced their parents to buy a croquet set after they have spent a few days with us. We won't outline the rules in detail here – the general aim is to move the ball through six hoops and hit the finishing post – but suggest you follow the basics reasonably strictly.

Lay out the hoops and posts on as large a space as you can find; our twist is that we deliberately play it on bumpy, sloping ground with a bit of long grass – for added annoyance. We usually have between two and four teams, so that each ball gets played by any number of people, according to how many of you there are. Four-a-side works well. The key thing is to split up the ages, sexes and abilities in order to make things fair and to avoid too many arguments. Players take it in strict turns and the game normally takes ages; it is improved if one or two teams gang up on others, though this has occasionally ended up in massive rows – typically with the males being accused of being too aggressive. I remember Caroline shouting this at me during one game, while waving a mallet dangerously close to my head. So be aware.

MAKING AND USING WEAPONS

~ CHARLIE ~

Ready, aim, fire ...!
Of all of the things we have
done with our children, building
and using hand-made weapons
(of the catapult rather than the
sawn-off shotgun variety, you
understand) has been just about
the most successful.

We have a theory that if all boys (and girls, to an extent, though in our experience they're less prone to the need to soak up violence) could spend some time wielding primitive weaponry, they'd cause a lot less trouble. It's something that puts that natural boyish energy to positive use, and the joy is that there is nothing goody-goody about it. The intention, of course, is never to hurt anyone; which is why they work so well in big, open spaces (or in a garden big enough to make them safe). Whether or not you agree, building and using these is fun.

A word of warning. These weapons can be very dangerous, and sensible adult supervision is necessary – keep them out of harm's way and out of reach of children so that they are not tempted to have a go when no adults are around. The one key lesson is that none of our Top Three Weapons should ever be aimed at anyone or at anything precious.

~ Potato cannon ~

This is the best, most dramatic weapon we have ever built. It works just like a real cannon but in miniature. We were introduced to the potato cannon by our American friend Frank Wood. He's a very successful businessman, but has dedicated his non-work life to being a big child. He built us one of these and sent it - from America - with a note that said: 'I have yet to see anyone - boy or girl, man or woman - fire one of these without laughing.' He was right. These are dangerous and brilliant fun. We have managed to fire a large chunk of potato over 300m. But, be careful.

WE'RE GOING
TO NEED A
BIGGER POTATO

~ You will need ~

A length of thick plastic pipe
  (about 1.75m long x 9cm in diameter
  and at least 7mm thick, probably more).
  One end must have a screw fitting
A junction box made of exactly the
  same material, with a screw fitting
  on each side

Two plastic screw caps to attach
  to the junction box above
The ignition system from a gas oven,
  which you can find in decent
  hardware stores
Some sealant or putty; the sort of thing
  you use in bathrooms is good
Some good-quality hairspray
Some large potatoes

~ How to build and use it ~

Sharpen one end of the long bit of
piping. To the other end – the one
with the screw fitting – connect the
junction box.

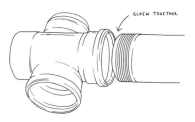

Drill a hole in one of the screw caps
and insert the ignition system; the
push button will need to be on the
outside of the cannon, the bit that
sparks should be on the inside. Seal
this, so that despite the hole you've
drilled, the whole thing is airtight.
Screw this section into position.
Put the other cap in position, like
this.

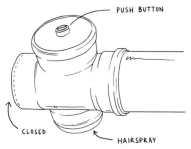

Right, now you have your cannon. You're ready for action. This next bit takes practice to get right.

1. *Push a potato into the cannon, at the open end of the barrel. The potato must be bigger than the chamber so that the sharpened end of the cannon trims it to fit snugly into the barrel. Push the potato right down the barrel, using a long, straight stick, until it rests just above the chamber that is created by the junction box – it needs to sit just above the chamber. Once you have managed this, mark the precise length that you have pushed the potato into the cannon on your stick; this will make it much easier to reload the cannon subsequently.*

2. *Unscrew the cap that doesn't have the ignition system in it. Then spray a quick burst of hairspray into the chamber. You'll get the quantity right by trial and error; you don't need much. The better quality the hairspray, the better the effect (quality here is probably best measured by price). Quickly replace the screw cap.*

3. *Check that no one is in your line of fire. Hold the cannon by your side and give the ignition system a good thwack. The spark ignites the gas and this propels the potato out of the cannon ... fast.*

Like so many things, this will take trial and error to get right. So, be patient.

Frank tells me that if you pierce a potato with a cocktail stick and soak it in alcohol overnight before firing it from your cannon, it will burn as it is fired and that this looks particularly impressive at night. I haven't tried this yet; I must get around to it.

~ Atlatl ~

The Atlatl (pronounced atalatal) is a highly effective dart launcher that will enable even relatively small children to lob a spear or dart about 100m. Atlatls were first used in the Upper Palaeolithic period (c.15,500 BC). Using them requires practice, but with time you will find them surprisingly efficient and accurate. These are every bit as lethal as the potato cannon; so be careful - keep them out of harm's way and out of reach of children so that they can't get at it or use without supervision.

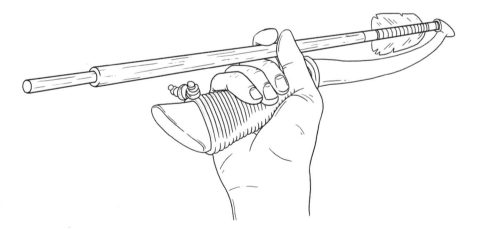

~ You will need ~

A strong branch for the Atlatl –
  about 0.5m long and 1.5cm in
  diameter. This can have a fork at
  one end that sits at 45 degrees to the
  main shaft and in the same plane.
  If you can't find something forked
  you'll need another small bit of wood
A piece of wood for the spear or arrow
  of about 0.5cm in diameter. Hazel is
  good for this because it is light and
  malleable. This should be a bit longer
  than the person who will be using the
  Atlatl is tall
A stone of about 3 x 2cm in diameter
A knife and some tape
Some feathers or plastic for the
  fletchings of your spear or arrow

1.

A BRANCH

TAPED BRANCH

2.

TAPE FLETCHINGS
TO BRANCH

~ How to build and use it ~

1. First, make the Atlatl by cutting the branch just above the fork. A forked branch will make the best, most stable weapon, but if you can't find a forked bit of wood attach another bit of wood to the end of the branch with the tape. This spur will hold the arrow or spear.

2. Tape the stone to the midsection of the Atlatl. This is not imperative, but it will result in a more forceful launch once you are an expert.

3. Now make your arrow. Sharpen one end ... remember kids: point that blade away from you! Then make the fletchings; these are not essential, but they help the spear or arrow to fly and make it look the business, too. Feather looks best, but using it is a real faff, so plastic is probably best; try an old plastic milk bottle. Cut three pieces and attach them with tape.

4. Prepare to be patient. Do not give up if the first few attempts are a disaster. Place the end of the arrow/spear into the spur that you created with the fork (or other piece of wood). Position both pieces of wood in the arch between your thumb and forefinger, holding the arrow/spear with your thumb and forefinger. Your hand should be near the end of the Atlatl. Now, throw. The motion that you need is a bit like lobbing a ball; swing the device over your shoulder, pull forward and flick.

5. Once you've mastered the art of the Atlatl you can choose a target to aim at. Make it a big one to begin with (such as a tree, for example, rather than your portly neighbour).

~ Archery ~

Years ago we bought a good bow and some arrows and had a lot of fun with them. Then they got put away, out of the reach of our children, and forgotten about until 2011, when archery became one of the big hits of the summer. And then our youngest, Felix, asked for some archery kit for Christmas, so, archery is now something we feel qualified to comment on.

Archery is an unfashionable sport, but goodness knows why; it is easy to learn, really satisfying and well suited to adults and children.

CAROLINE!

~ You will need ~

First select good kit. There is beginner's kit and adult's kit and children's kit and highly expensive kit; so you need to be sure that you are buying the right thing. If in doubt, ask a pro.

Essentially there are two types of bow; the compound bow is the elaborate one that looks like something from one of those fantasy/war video games. And while it does offer more power relative to the archer's draw, there is also a lot more to go wrong with it. The recurve is the simple, classic, elegant bow and although this requires more power to draw than the compound bow, we prefer this. (Technically, there is also the long bow, but that's a bit specialist for us or these pages.)

Then select your arrows. There are loads of different types; aluminium, carbon or wooden shafts come with all sorts of heads. Our recommendation here is to go for something cheap because you will break and/or lose most of them. And, buy as many as you can

afford; it is incredibly frustrating to lose your last unbroken arrow just as you are getting the hang of things.

Then you'll need a decent target and something to hold it in place. And finally, we recommend an arm guard: they are easy to find and quite cheap. I am not quite sure why it happens sometimes and doesn't others, but when the bow's string thwacks the inside of your arm it really hurts.

~ How to do it ~

Firing an arrow is surprisingly easy (easier then using a catapult, in fact). As you place the arrow's notch in the bow's string make sure that the bow is parallel to the ground. Once the arrow is in place, raise the bow until it is at about 90 degrees to the ground and you can look down the arrow without moving your head. Stay relaxed. Now - quickly, or you will get tired - draw the string back and look down the arrow and through the notch in the bow. Release. Repeat. With practice you'll soon become surprisingly accurate.

~ Catapult ~

Naughty, great fun and as old as the hills. The catapult is the most simple to make of our top three, but pretty good, nonetheless. We did some bad stuff to windows with ours when we were young but, of course, we strongly advise against this. More recently, we have spent many happy hours with our children chucking stones into the river with catapults.

~ You will need ~

A solid branch in the shape of a Y, ideally about 20-25cm high and 2cm in diameter
A good knife, some scissors and a bicycle inner tube
Some ammo: small pebbles are good, and again only in wide open spaces or a garden large enough to enable them to be thrown safely

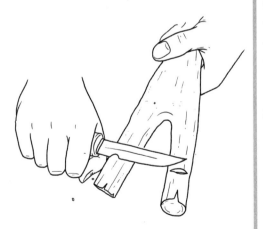

~ How to build and use it ~

1. First, cut two notches in the Y of wood (see illustration). Remember, cut with the blade facing away from you (this seems elementary, but you'd be surprised).

2. Cut a slice of bicycle inner tube (with scissors) that is 50-60cm long and 1cm wide. Leave a circular holder (for ammo) of about 2cm wide at the midpoint of the tube. Attach the tube to the notches in the Y with a strong knot.

3. Choose your ammo, check that no one is in the line of fire, then pull back and fire. Do not be embarrassed when your first few shots just fall to the ground. Be confident and relaxed and you'll be amazed how far you can hurl stuff.

GOOD THINGS FOR THE CHILDREN TO DO OUTSIDE

- CHARLIE -

~ Make rosehip itching powder ~

Rosehips look lovely and can be put to masses of uses; they're good for jelly and one friend of ours used to make cordial with them.

The wild rose, or dog rose grows in profusion in hedgerows and on overgrown sunny banks. They flower with a lovely pale pink or white bloom in early summer, and by autumn the bright, glossy hips glow with a distinctive pinky-red colour and are almost oval.

Rosehip jelly and cordial are all very well, but they are not as good as itching powder. And rosehips are probably the best source of itching powder in the great British outdoors. Our children once put it down their headmaster's bed when he came to stay with us. We were trying to suck up to him; this might not have helped. He didn't say anything.

~ How to do it ~

Making rosehip itching powder is easy. It is most potent if the berries have been dried for a week or two in a warm place, say an airing cupboard, on a sheet of newspaper, but perfectly effective from fresh berries. All you do is break open the berry and extract the insides: the fine hairs and the seeds. And there you have your itching powder. We always used to spoon it out but it's fine to use fingers, too - just make sure you wash your hands afterwards or you'll be inflicting an itch on yourself. The powder is best applied down the back of someone's neck. It's quite a mild itch, but still, a word of caution; avoid attacking people with sensitive skin or eczema.

~ Conker fighting ~

Collecting conkers from underneath horse chestnut trees and using them to fight with occupied endless hours of our childhood. It was one of the best things about autumn and used to consume break times with ease at school. It's probably banned now at most schools on health and safety grounds, which makes it an even more worthwhile thing to do. Maybe you or your children should try reintroducing it at school because it really is good fun. Yes, there is a risk that you might thwack someone in the face or on their hand; but the whole point of the game is to be accurate – and there are some tips on that below.

~ How to do it ~

First things first: find a good conker. It must have fallen from the tree to be ready for fighting. Next, make a hole through your conker. A metal skewer is best but be careful not to slip and put a hole in your hand instead. The best way to go about it is to put the conker on a semi-hard surface (like a piece of cork or grass) before slowly piercing the conker with your skewer. The smaller the hole the stronger the remaining conker; the stronger the conker, the better for fighting (for tips on making yours harder, see the 'ways to doctor conkers' tips, below). Thread a string through the hole you've made, and tie a knot at the bottom; thick trainer laces are best because thin string can hurt your hand and/or cut through the conker. Laces are also easiest to thread as they are hard at the ends. The lace/string should be about 30cm long.

Now, you are ready to fight an opponent. The object is simple: to smash your friend's conker before they smash yours. Toss a coin to decide who starts. Then take it in turns to take a swing at each other's conker. One fighter dangles their conker, holding it at chest height, away from their body. When it is still, their opponent swings their conker – overarm – onto the swinging one. If they hit it, that's good; they get another go. If they miss, not so good; it's the other fighter's go. For extra accuracy, keep your string good and short as you swing and don't be too ambitious with the distance or speed of your swing.

This carries on until one conker is smashed off its string. Not cracked, but smashed right off. The winning conker then attains a score; if this is its first victory it is a one-er, its second a two-er and so on. We used to have conkers that went well above hundred-ers. Sometimes we retired them because they were so special. And sometimes – just sometimes – we cheated a little by adding fake scores to new conkers.

There are three categories of game. First, you can both agree to play with fresh, first-year conkers; ones that you have just picked up. Second, you can agree to play with doctored conkers. And, third, you can agree to play with fresh conkers but cheat by doctoring yours in undetectable ways.

~ Ways to doctor conkers ~

▶ *Soak your conker in vinegar until the skin starts to wrinkle. Be aware that a wrinkled skin is detectable if you intend to cheat. Another consequence of pickling a conker is that the insides can rot, which is not good. So, a week in vinegar should do.*

▶ *Varnish your conker. If you are planning on cheating, beware that this can be easy to detect; a matt finish rather than a gloss finish varnish is easier to disguise.*

▶ *Bake your conker in an oven at very low heat overnight. This can be highly effective. Apparently, if you then rub your conker with moisturising cream this makes it even stronger, but we have not tried this yet.*

▶ *Use a conker from a previous year. Those that are a year old are best. Do not make a hole until you are ready to use your conker.*

▶ *Beware that a hard conker can be a brittle conker. As ever, trial, error and practice make perfect.*

~ Tree climbing ~

I spent entire school holidays climbing trees. We had one huge cypress near to our house that was particularly good to climb; we had to use a rope ladder to reach the first branch but once we were inside the canopy it was a doddle, with loads of different routes to the top. Poking our heads out of the canopy at the top was always thrilling. We used to climb giant yews, too. These were good because we always felt safe inside them; if you slipped, the dense network of branches was bound to catch you, even if hitting a branch hurt. This safety thing is important; weirdly enough, tree climbing is probably the most dangerous thing that we'll advocate in this book.

If you look on the Internet you'll find lots of tips about climbing trees with helmets, ropes and harnesses; and lots of places that you can do it in a supervised way. This sounds great fun; but I don't think that there was anything except free, DIY climbing when I was little. And this is the best way because all you do is spot a tree and, well, climb it.

There is only one way to decide on the best tree; and that is to look at it and see if it looks good for climbing. Dense trees are good for beginners for reasons already stated; small trees can be lots of fun, as being only 6m off the ground can be exhilarating without there being too far to fall. All sorts of pine trees are good, as are oak, beech, plane and yew. But, really, if you can get onto the first branch you can climb the rest of the tree. Use a rope ladder (I wouldn't bother trying to make one yourself, they're very easy to buy) or a rope or a friend's shoulders to get up to that branch.

Though it's impossible to take the risk out of tree climbing, here are some tips to help a little . . .

▶ *Start on small trees.*

▶ *Be cautious! Your friend who is fearless and almost runs up the tree is not the best climber.*

▶ *Go slowly, check a branch for stability with your hands before you climb onto it.*

▶ *Stay as close to the tree's trunk as you can. Branches are weaker the further from the trunk you go; and if one snaps it very rarely does so right up to the trunk, so you should be able to retain a foot hold even as most of the branch hits the ground.*

▶ *Do not be too ambitious. Practice makes perfect.*

▶ *Go down the same way you went up, facing inwards, like climbing down a ladder, not like going down stairs.*

▶ *Going down is harder than going up. So, as you climb, remember that.*

▶ *If you are climbing with someone, make sure you don't tread on their fingers – particularly as you climb down and if you're behind (and therefore, above) them. This can lead to them letting go and falling.*

▶ *Don't carve stuff in trees to commemorate your ascent, or use nails or anything similar to attach ropes. (In the section on 'dens', p.111, you can read why – it's not just about looking after the trees.)*

~ Rope swings ~

Rope swings are brilliant. One summer when I was about ten we built one over a rocky river in Scotland, which was fun but incredibly dangerous. You do not want to land on rocks - it's best to have a mossy, leafy place to land, or deep water. This is as much fun for adults as it is for children.

Whether planning to jump off your swing onto land or water, or just swoop around, the construction of the swing is essentially the same.

~ How to do it ~

1. First, buy a good length of thick, natural rope; the synthetic stuff might last longer, but it looks nasty and burns your hands.

2. Tie a big knot in one end, or attach a tyre or chunk of wood.

3. Find the right tree; this is by far and away the most difficult bit. A tree on a bank that leans in the direction of your forward swing is best. And the branch that you plan to attach the swing to should, ideally, be perpendicular to the direction of swing. Saw or chop off any branches that might obstruct your swing; remember that you might swing around quite wildly in all directions, so make sure you have clear swinging space within several feet of the perfect line of swinging.

4. Sling the other end over the branch and knot it. The better the knot the safer the swing (see p.44, for different types of knots). You can also use a pulley to aid smooth movement.

5. Finally, swing.

There is a magical scene in one of the best films of all time, *Son of Rambow* (a coming-of-age story set in the 1980s, about two schoolboy friends), where the hero drops from a huge rope swing into deep water only to reveal that he can't swim. There are two lessons here: if you are going to land in water, test for a deep spot before putting up your swing. And if you are with a group of lots of kids, make sure they can all swim first.

~ Making smoke signals ~

We used to make smoke signals in our games as children. They seemed like the very coolest things that North American Indians did (although I believe that they were first used on the Great Wall of China) and they were surprisingly easy to achieve. We used to make up a language and see if we could decipher each other's signals.

You need to work in pairs, at least two, three or more pairs is even better, and you need to build at least two small smoky fires to have the most fun; add damp leaves or bunches of grass or, best of all, heather to a good, strong fire. It is best to try this on a reasonably still day, so that you don't need huge amounts of smoke, and to light the fires on open or hilly ground.

Once the first fire is smoking, hold a small bit of thick, damp blanket (or an old bit of carpet, dampened with water is ideal) between you both over it and then quickly move the blanket to release a puff of smoke. The blanket or carpet shouldn't be at risk of catching fire; you need to have a very smoky fire which, by definition, shouldn't have too much flame. The language is up to you; three small puffs might mean 'hello', two bigger ones 'whistle if you can read this'.

Historically, tribes would, of course, have had their own language, but nothing is set – it's just fun. (Besides, you'll probably want to say more than 'bison on the move' or 'danger, white man coming'.)

Persevere and you'll soon get the hang of it and you can have competitions to find the best signaller.

BUILDING DAMS AND DENS

~ Dams ~

We both absolutely loved building dams when we were children. It's still good fun - delightfully pointless, fun: you build something, get wet, get dirty, get tired and hungry - wonderful. It is also probably gently educational, but that isn't the aim; this is a simple mission to beat the river.

As you get more practised you will be able to build more and more elaborate dams. The challenge is to make something elegant and efficient.

Pick a small river or a part of a river that is narrow. Don't be too ambitious. Start with the biggest rocks you can manage and drop these into the water as the foundations of the dam: ideally they will span the width of the river. Then use smaller rocks and top these with clods of earth and grass (a spade is useful at this point). Assuming that your dam is efficient, at some point you'll need to create a run-off channel so the water doesn't rise too high behind the dam and flow over the top (turning your dam into a weir).

That's it really. Simple, uncomplicated, WET fun.

~ Dens ~

Building a den is equally delightful, and possibly a bit more rewarding, too. This simple activity often occupied us for entire weeks when we were children. Every year our dens would become more elaborate and ingenious. I don't think I could offer instructions as to how to build a den because pretty much the point is that you just build with what's available. The best dens are the most elaborate; there's an absolute joy in making something that's reasonably complicated with, say, a roof, or different rooms, or big enough to fit a few of you into it.

There are two rules, though, if you are building a den in a wood or other wild area, rather than at the back of the garden.

The first contradicts what I suspect those who write the Countryside Code would suggest, namely that you break up the den when you have finished. Indeed I recently saw a guide to the countryside that suggested that you break up your den when you have finished

playing in it and 'scatter the materials around in as natural a way as possible' . . . ! (Just how does one 'scatter in a natural way'? It doesn't mean anything, and this, to us, is exactly the way the countryside *shouldn't* be treated.) So I disagree, leave your den as it is; then other people can enjoy it and - best of all - you can return later in the year and see how it has fared.

Second, never, ever, hammer nails into trees. Not only will these damage the tree but they are lethal if someone ever comes to saw the tree; nails can snap chainsaws and consequently injure or kill people. Indeed, some radical forest protection groups make use of this fact in their activism, by hammering long nails into certain trees and then telling the logging firms what they have done - but without telling them which trees are spiked . . .

BUILDING A RAFT

'It's lovely to live on a raft. We had the sky up there, all speckled with stars, and we used to lay on our backs and look up at them, and discuss about whether they was made or only just happened ... Other places do seem so cramped up and smothery, but a raft don't.'
Mark Twain

When I was about 11, my brother, sister and various friends spent a week building rafts on a summer holiday in Scotland. It was brilliant fun but the rafts were spectacularly unsuccessful and capsized as soon as we tried to get onto them - our mistake was building them to look good on dry land. As soon as they hit the water all the design problems revealed themselves at once - it's much harder to get them to balance than you might imagine. The next year we made better, more stable rafts - purely by being patient and methodical, rather than just excited. And the third year we managed to build one that actually worked. Since then we have built various pretty efficient rafts.

There is a very primitive pleasure about floating downstream on a raft that you have built yourself - and a raft is the sort of thing that you have to make; it just doesn't feel right buying one.

With a little bit of forward planning, a basic raft is also extremely simple to construct (as long as, unlike us, you don't start out just making it up as you go along).

Below are my instructions for a large raft. But you can just as easily scale everything down to make a smaller, four-barrel raft.

~ You will need ~

Six large (200–220 litre) plastic barrels. These are readily available on the Internet. Ideally, get hold of something unused; when we built our first rafts we 'borrowed' some metal barrels from a local sawmill; I dread to think what was/had been in them

Seven good, thick, but small tree trunks. These can be bought from any wood yard; it's best to get them cut to the right size once you have found your barrels

Masses of thin, strong rope (at least 50m long, but you can't have too much)

Long nails, a hammer, maybe a saw

At least two oars or paddles or even a pole for punting

~ How to build and use it ~

Whatever you do, make your raft close to water. It isn't going to be easy to drag it around.

The key thing I've discovered is to build the frame first, and then lash the barrels on top of it: those early attempts with my siblings involved trying to place the barrels under the wooden frame, which is how one imagines a raft should look. However, stability will be massively aided by doing what may feel counterintuitive – because it looks like you're making the raft upside down – and having the barrels on top of the frame. And passengers will be able to stay dry(ish) by sitting on top of the barrels.

1. First, lash the trunks together to create a four-sided wooden frame with slightly overlapping corners (so you have something to lash to – see p.44 to choose the right knot to use). Use nails too for extra stability – hammering them into the corners before you start with the rope. You'll need two pairs of hands for the best results.

Use your barrels to create the precise dimensions of the frame; they should fit snugly inside it.

2. You'll also need to add two trunks in the middle to stabilise the frame; attach these in the same way as earlier – using nails first and then knots.

3. Next, lash the barrels into place.

4. Make sure that they are held firmly because they'll undergo much more strain than you might imagine.

5. Now launch the raft and get on. Someone will fall in. Maybe you all will. But you'll get the hang of it.

Finally, we also once made a good smaller raft out of car inner tubes, some rope and a sheet of plywood. It was mildly successful. And we even made one for Action Man out of some wood and ping-pong balls, but that didn't really work – but the fun was in the building. Or, at least, that's what we told ourselves as we watched Action Man slowly sinking . . .

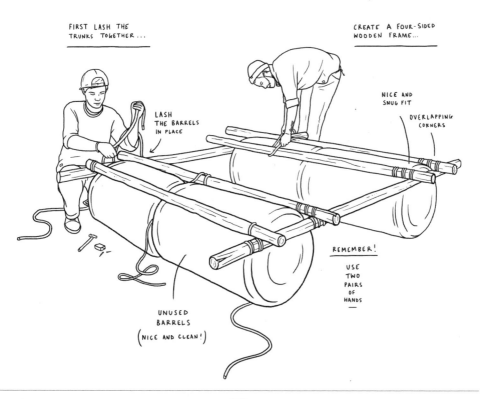

FIRST LASH THE
TRUNKS TOGETHER . . .

CREATE A FOUR-SIDED
WOODEN FRAME . . .

NICE AND
SNUG FIT

OVERLAPPING
CORNERS

LASH
THE BARRELS
IN PLACE

REMEMBER!

USE
TWO
PAIRS
OF
HANDS

UNUSED
BARRELS
(NICE AND CLEAN!)

MEASURING THE HEIGHT OF A TREE

~ CAROLINE ~

How often have we all looked at a particularly tall tree and idly wondered how tall it is?

When we first moved to Scotland from London in April 1990, we essentially had to camp for the first month or so, because there had been a series of unavoidable hitches with the builders. During the first week of what some of our friends considered to be self-imposed exile, our great friend Gavin came up on the train from London with his bicycle. The morning after he arrived, he looked out of the window and spotted a majestically tall Wellingtonia tree on the other side of the River Dye, which runs below the house. 'How tall is that tree?' he asked. Neither of us had any idea, and made an educated guess, but that wasn't good enough for Gavin. He needed to know. So Gavin took out his bike and set off for Banchory, around ten miles away, to procure a protractor.

A couple of hours later, pencil, paper and protractor in hand, Gavin set off over the bridge 'to triangulate the tree'. Half an hour later, he had his answer.

~ How do you triangulate a tree? ~

There are two ways: both require a protractor, but only an elemental memory of geometry.

~ Method 1: you will need ~

A protractor

A piece of string, around 40cm long,
   weighted with a pencil rubber
   or similar

Sticky tape

~ How to do it ~

Thread the string through the hole in the middle of the flat edge of the protractor. Tie a knot at one end to secure it there. Attach the rubber (or something else small and weighted) to the other end so that it becomes a plumb line.

Holding the protractor pointing towards the tree, with its straight edge parallel to the ground at eye level (and the curved edge pointing downwards), walk backwards away from the tree in a straight line until the angle from your eye to the top of the tree is 45 degrees, and bring the edge of the protractor up to follow your eyeline.

You can check the angle with the piece of string, which will be hanging down marking it. Mark where you're standing on the ground when you've reached the 45-degrees point, and then pace out the distance from that spot to the base of the tree. This distance, plus the distance from your eye to the ground is equal to the height of the tree.

~ Method 2: you will need ~

A protractor

A fat drinking straw

Clear sticky tape

Some string (around 40cm long)

A pencil rubber

A friend

~ How to do it ~

1. This is a somewhat brainier method. Attach the weighted string to the protractor as described in method 1. Now, using the clear sticky tape, attach the straw along the straight edge, with a bit of straw overhanging either side. (Be careful not to squish the straw as you will shortly need to look through it, like a telescope.)

2. Standing a good distance from the tree, hold the protractor with its straight edge parallel to the floor and its curved edge pointing downwards. Bring it up so it is level with your eye and look up at the tree through the straw which, along with the protractor, will now be tilting upwards. When you can see the top of the tree through it, get your friend to check and write down the angle that the string is marking out on the protractor.

3. Now – before you move! – get the friend to also measure the distance from your feet to the bottom of the tree, or mark it and do it yourself.

4. To calculate the height of the tree, use similar triangles: on a piece of paper, use the protractor to draw a right-angled triangle with the same angle at **a** as the angle you measured from the tree. The base of the triangle, **d**, represents the distance from the point at which you measured the angle to the base of the tree. And the side of the triangle, **h**, represents the height of the tree.

5. This triangle can now be scaled to the whole tree: measure the height (**h**) and base (**d**) of the triangle you have just drawn. To calculate the height of the tree, multiply the number you get from that sum (**h** divided by **d**) by the distance from the point at which you measured the angle to the base of the tree (**D**). Add the distance from your eye to the ground (**e**), and you have the height of the tree (**H**). In other words:

$$H = D \times (h \div d) + e$$

IF ONLY!

Gavin used the second method, which is more complicated but more accurate. Did he get it right? To within half a metre or so, according to someone we met the following week who knew the tree well.

BUILDING A SCARECROW

- CHARLIE -

Scarecrows have existed, in endless different forms and in most agricultural societies, for a very long time, as a device to frighten hungry birds away from crops. Over 2,500 years ago the Greeks are thought to have made scarecrows in the image of Priapus – the son of Dionysus and Aphrodite – as he was exceptionally ugly and therefore efficient as a deterrent to hungry birds. The Romans copied the Greeks' scarecrows and spread the idea widely across Europe. In Britain, boys were often used as live scarecrows. And Japan's oldest book, *Kojiki*, written in the early 700s, includes a god-like scarecrow called Kuebiko who knows everything there is to know about Earth. Today scarecrows are still widely used and have featured in many (often spooky), films and books for all ages.

We once had an online build-a-scarecrow competition at Pedlars and had masses of incredibly imaginative entries. I think a brilliant Jimi Hendrix won. Building a scarecrow is a creative challenge and a practical one too, especially if you have some young seedlings or fruit to protect in your garden or field. A scarecrow-making competition would be good for a party of older children, or a great weekend project with younger kids. They are pretty simple to make.

~ You will need ~

A couple of bits of wood:
  a 1.8m plank (which must be narrower than a trouser-leg) and a broomstick cut down by 30cm or so, are ideal. But anything of similar length will do
A hammer and a couple of longish nails
Half a small square bale of hay or straw
A spade
Some string
A square of hessian, or a hessian sack, big enough to create your scarecrow's head from
As many clothes, including long trousers and a jumper or long-sleeved shirt, as you can muster. A hat, gloves and scarf are good additions
Any other bits and pieces you can find. Maybe a pipe or a guitar

~ How to do it ~

1. First, nail the pieces of wood together to form a cross; the broomstick for the arms, the plank for the body.

2. Tie the ends of the trousers and shirt or jumper together and stuff them quite generously with hay or straw. Leave one trouser-leg only loosely tied – you'll need to untie it later.

3. Fill the hessian square or sack with hay/straw; if you can, cut and sew this into an oval shape: it'll make a great head, but a square stuffed with hay/straw and gathered and tied by the four corners at one end – like a balloon – will do fine. Don't be too particular anyway; the result will be rough and ready, but the overall effect is what matters. And that will be good.

4. Now, tie the head to the collar of the shirt using the string but leaving a small opening just big enough to accommodate your piece of wood and then ram these onto the top of the wooden cross, manipulating the arms of the shirt over the broomstick.

If you can't manage this, and it depends on the length of your broomstick versus the size of your shirt, you can tie the floppy scarecrow's arms onto the broomstick, so that it looks a bit like he/she has been crucified. But this doesn't make for as professional a result.

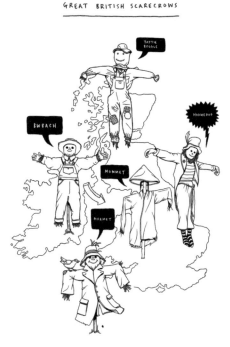

5. Next, post the plank down one leg of the trousers; the one that you tied loosely when you were stuffing it. Feed it out at the bottom of the leg, leaving enough length to bury into the ground sturdily enough for your scarecrow to stand up. Tie the leg up again.

6. Now add gloves for hands, a jacket, maybe a scarf, straw or hay for hair, a hat, a face, whatever. This is the really creative bit.

7. Dig a hole deep enough to hold your scarecrow upright, stick the scarecrow into it and pack with earth until it stands stable.

8. Stand back and admire.

BUILDING A TREEHOUSE

~ WILLIAM GLADSTONE ~

Charlie's dad has built endless treehouses, some more successful than others, but they are always elaborate, imaginative, multi-roomed and mildly bonkers. Here, he explains how to do it.

'I have built a few treehouses in my day and have learnt from my mistakes. I have built each one of them because it presented a challenge, and because I would have loved to have one as a child. I never did, although once a couple of my cousins and I took possession of a whole load of our uncle's fencing timber which was stacked in his orchard at his home in Cheshire, and built a hut overnight (literally) using the materials available.

'The grown-ups were so impressed that they did not insist on demolishing it to recover the timber, and it stood there for some years as an ideal headquarters for our adventures. It had no windows but it was waterproof and private. It gave me the confidence to realise that building a wooden house was not too difficult.

'The reason for this escapade was that another uncle had bought his son a very grand hut in kit form which we thought was much too smart to be tolerated. You will at once realise that what follows is not for professionals, but for amateurs who want to "have a go", but aren't sure how to start.'

~ How to do it and what to use ~

~ Using timber ~

You may be satisfied with getting hold of the cheapest bits of timber you can lay your hands on, perhaps by cadging waste from a builder or going to a sawmill and asking for the slab wood. In both cases they will probably be happy to have it taken away, because waste disposal is an expensive business nowadays. If they give you a flea in the ear because people are endlessly begging them for firewood, please don't blame me. Slab wood, by the way, is the four rounded outside edges that have to be discarded before you can saw a tree into boards. It makes a good rustic fence, but if you want to use it to clad a building you may have to do a lot of straightening up of the edges.

The cheapest way of getting good boards for the floor, walls and perhaps even the roof is to buy Yorkshire boards from an agricultural merchant. These are the boards you often see on big livestock sheds on farms, usually to clad the ends of these buildings. The boards are erected with gaps of about 25mm between them so as to ensure good ventilation, but they serve pretty well for the walls of a treehouse if pushed together (or 'butted up' as a joiner would say).

For all the other timber I would go to a big fencing contractor. You will probably get pretty well everything you need, with the great advantage that it has been pressure-treated (tanalised) and won't rot for very many years. It is a pale, greenish-brown rather neutral colour. It is not as nice as larch (see below), but it looks quite good. The Yorkshire boards will also be tanalised.

The best timber is larch. It needs no treatment of any kind, and lasts for donkey's years. It goes a nice silvery-grey. But any timber will do. The Norwegians, unsurprisingly, use Norway spruce. They use it horizontally to clad their houses. I prefer to use larch vertically. Butt the boards up against each other and then nail on thinner bits to cover the joins. This may sound amateurish but it isn't: it's the old vernacular way, especially in Scotland, and it looks good and makes a building wind- and waterproof. Whether you use larch or not, vertical boarding is still a good idea, preferably with the thin bits nailed on to cover the gaps.

Whatever sort of treehouse you make, you will need to attach it to the tree and how to do this will probably answer itself when you have found the perfect location. Sometimes I lash the construction to the tree with strong rope, or bolt it on, or even nail it into place.

~ Other materials ~

You can use steel or plastic sheets for the roof but I prefer timber. Perspex is good for windows but tricky to cut. If you buy it from a plastics specialist they will cut it for you. Right-angled metal corner joiners from a builder's merchant are ideal for fixing the walls to the floor and perhaps the roof to the walls. A battery-driven screwdriver or cordless drill and suitable screws will save a great deal of energy, time and agony, especially

for fitting these corner joiners. Buy the screws in boxes from a builder's merchant. Drywall screws are particularly good because their ends are sharp and they start easily.

~ Tools and equipment ~

Tape measure, set square, spirit level, pencil, saw, hammer, nails, pliers for removing bosh shots, ladder, rope or string and a bit of imagination.

Now as to ladders, be extremely careful. Make sure the ground surface is flat, or level it with big bits of wood. Get somebody to stand on the bottom rung. Tie the ladder to the tree or to something equally secure if necessary. Don't cut off the branch that supports the ladder: I know this sounds stupid but it has been the cause of many fatal accidents.

However, if a ladder is properly erected it is most unlikely that children, even small children, will fall off it. This is obviously a residual skill from our prehensile past. Tell them not to look down and, above all, insist that when they want to come down they come out of the treehouse and on to the ladder BACKWARDS. Never let them come out forwards. Be very firm over this discipline, and all will be well. Children, even small ones, are much safer than many grown-ups. To train them, go up the ladder immediately behind them and come down in front of them.

~ A few basic hints ~

Get the floor built first. Then you can use it as a platform for the rest of the job. Time spent getting it level is never wasted. Standard fencing rails about 1.2m x 500mm are ideal for the framework. If you cut your own timber, use 1.2m x 600mm. The floor is the only weight-bearing part, so use the rails upright, not on their sides, about 30cm apart and as near parallel to each other as conditions allow. Join each one to its neighbour with a short length of the same timber here and there to add strength. Fix rails round the outside to complete the job. Then nail on the floorboards.

Now build the framework for each wall. Use roughly 600 x 600mm wood (or better still 600 x 900mm as it is easier to bang in the nails without splitting the wood). These timbers can well be about 60cm apart. Leave appropriate spaces for doors and windows. Fix the wall frameworks to the floor, using metal joiners, fastened by screws driven by a battery-driven screwdriver. Don't nail on the wall cladding yet.

To keep the whole treehouse rigid it is absolutely essential to have one diagonal timber firmly fixed to at least two of the four walls (i.e., one wall in each of two dimensions). It needn't go from corner to corner and it doesn't need to be at 45 degrees, but it must join two of the outside edges of the wall frameworks. If you don't do this, your house may blow into a very funny shape during the first gale.

Put the roof on before you put the cladding on the walls.

When you lean out to nail the cladding on the walls, use a safety belt.

~ Suitable sites ~

~ A hollow tree ~

I suppose a true treehouse is a house in a hollow tree like the one Owl (or Wol) occupies in *Winnie-the-Pooh*. I have built a couple of these, one in an ash tree and one in a huge sycamore, but the trouble is that, even if you have a suitable tree, the house is too small except for little children (or owls). In the first one I built in the old ash tree you could get in through a rotten bit at the top so you first had to climb a ladder and then to descend another ladder to floor level, which made it quite exciting. To get any degree of comfort, you need to put in a wooden floor: keep it a few centimetres off the ground for dryness and warmth. This house needed a bit of patching in the roof and some sort of lamp. It could have taken an upper floor but I never put one in. It was not very comfortable but it had the advantage of being spooky and secret.

The second one (in the sycamore) had a hole in the trunk at the bottom: a ready-made front door on the ground floor. With a few bits of furniture and equipment it made a good playhouse for small children.

~ My best effort: a huge ash stump ~

It must be very rare to find a huge tree that has been cut off well above ground level, but this makes the absolutely ideal site for a genuine treehouse. I had the luck to have one in the garden. The reason was that this had been an ancient specimen ash tree, and when it started to get dangerous by rotting at the top nobody could bear to cut it right down. So it was cut about 6m from the ground and then started to sprout again round the new top.

The flat trunk where it had been cut off gave me a platform to start from. The new branches had grown quite big. I cut off all the weaker ones and cantilevered the floor of the house out over the void below, supporting it here and there on one of the remaining new branches. The difficulty was that some of these new branches had grown upright so I had to accommodate two of them inside the treehouse. It was practically impossible to make the holes watertight, but that didn't matter too much because the drops of water liked to cling to the trunk.

These branches inside the house were very awkward to build round, but they added character. It is the height of fashion to have a tree in your conservatory, the bigger the better if you want to impress the neighbours. (It is not so good to have one growing in the drawing room; usually this is a sign that the maintenance bills have got beyond your resources. In that case you might do best to downsize: perhaps by building a treehouse in the garden.)

The framework for the floor can be made of standard fencing rails which measure about 1.2m x 500mm. The important timbers are the load-bearing ones, i.e. the floor. They must lie upright, that is to say with the longer side vertical, and they should be about 30cm apart. However, depending on the shape of the tree you can vary the distances between them. Make sure they are level by putting bits of timber under them as wedges where necessary. Nail a rail round the edges of the framework and if necessary saw bits to go between two rails here and there to strengthen the structure. Then nail on the floorboards. If you get the timber sawn specially then the timbers can be 1.2m x 600mm, a little more robust than standard fencing rails.

'I love this treehouse because Grandpa built it, and he built it so well and so strongly that I am not afraid to climb to the top floor. And I have to climb to the top floor because this is where my cousin Piers and I can go to escape from his little sister, or boring adult conversations.'
Felix Gladstone, 11 years old

~ A big tree ~

The next best thing is a house built in a huge tree where it branches out and you can find a place to put a platform to serve as the floor. Again, this sort of treehouse is rather small but you can cantilever it out so that the outer edges have no apparent means of support. Or, better still, you can make it more than one storey high. This makes it look good and exciting to be in, but the shape has to follow the shape of the tree, more or less, so you can't work from a plan but just have to design it as you go along, using the method described above.

~ Several trees growing close together ~

This is probably the most common site for a really splendid treehouse, and it is much easier to build than the ones I have described above. It can be designed to the size you want. How good it looks will depend more on its design than on its site, so give this some thought. Generous eaves and, if there is a balcony, a neat handrail will help. You will still have to begin by building the platform. Start by erecting strong joists of timber between the trees. You will probably need something bigger than fencing rails, with dimensions 1.8m or even 2.4m x 600mm, depending on how far apart they are.

~ A house round the trunk of a large tree ~

This is a very popular kind of treehouse, easy to build except the actual surrounding of the tree, and comfortable to use – suitable even for the grown-ups to settle themselves in deckchairs for a drink on a summer evening. It can be supported on beams at each corner and it can have a staircase rather than a ladder. It looks attractive in the garden and presents no challenge to the builder except skill in joinery.

~ Treehouses with bridges or climbing frames ~

These are not suited to the average, or even the bigger than average garden, but if you have a wooded area and a large family they may fit your needs.

~ A peculiar one ~

I started with Wendy houses: the smallest was demountable and was designed to be carried through a small terraced house in London, and the largest was a terrace of three 'semis' in a remote part of Scotland. The first treehouse I built for our three children was erected on a small island where three alder trees had grown with their stumps very close together and their trunks leaning outwards. This was the most unusual three-storey treehouse I ever built. The bottom house was obviously the smallest. It was extremely difficult to erect the roof over the top house. I did it by using feather-boarding, with each board at a slightly different angle from its neighbour. Architecturally it was the most attractive treehouse I have ever made.

There were two snags. Firstly, our middle child wouldn't permit our eldest to pass through her premises to gain access to his own top floor. This I solved by erecting a rather hair-raising ladder. Secondly, the house needed to stretch in a gale. However, it lasted for quite a few years.

'This treehouse has gone now, erased by the passage of time and the weather. I always look for it when I row past this island; hoping that something will remain. But it doesn't. I absolutely loved it and I wish it was still there, as fresh, magical and original as the day it was completed.' **Charlie**

CAMPING

Notes

_____
_____
_____
_____
_____
_____
_____
_____
_____
_____
_____
_____
_____
_____
_____
_____
_____
_____
_____
_____
_____
_____
_____
_____
_____
_____

OUR TOP FIVE TENTS

- CHARLIE -

'It always rains on tents. Rainstorms will travel thousands of miles, against prevailing winds for the opportunity to rain on a tent.' **Dave Barry**

~ Pop-up tents ~
Best for the easy life

If you're heading to a festival, or planning to pitch your tent in the dark, then the pop-up tent is a good thing. Using ours still feels a little bit like cheating, but, well, we can live with that.

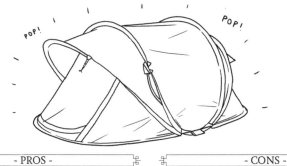

- PROS -	- CONS -
They are ridiculously easy to put up – and (almost) as easy to take down.	*They're ugly as sin – and made from nylon so, once the sun is up, you'll roast (not good if you're hung-over).*
They are cheap – and reliable because they always flip up very quickly.	*Lightweight yes, small no – they are large and therefore generally cumbersome, even when folded 'down', due to the construction of the pop-up frame.*
They travel well – because they're so lightweight.	

~ The tipi (or, sometimes, teepee) ~
Best for garden camping

We have a tipi, which we erect at the start of the summer and use as a spare room. We've had it for over a decade and it is still immaculate. Tipis were originally made of animal skins by nomadic North American Indians; now they are generally made of canvas. The word tipi comes from Siouan, which is spoken by the Lakota people of the Sioux tribes. It's great in the garden as it's not something you can easily transport about – so somewhere where it will be in situ for some time or even a permanent structure is ideal.

~ PROS ~	~ CONS ~
They're stylish – tipis are the most elegant tents in the world. They are made of canvas, wood and – generally – natural fibre rope; so, not a shred of sweaty nylon in sight.	*They are not easy to transport – tipis are incredibly heavy. In addition to the huge canvas skin and liner, there are 15 or 16 (depending on the type of tipi) very long poles.*
They're flame-friendly – you can light an open fire and cook in a tipi, using the smoke flaps at the top.	*They're a nightmare to put up – it can take an hour or so and the method is very precise and complicated. We generally have a row when we're putting ours up.*
Endurance – a good tipi should last forever.	*They are expensive – a good tipi starts at about £2000.*

~ The cabin tent ~
Best for families

This is the tent to go for if you want multiple rooms. We had one when we were children and we used to camp in it by a lake in Anglesey. It got blown away once with all of our stuff in it; but we found it pretty quickly, hiding behind a high wall. Cabin tents are widely available and second-hand versions are often available at eBay.

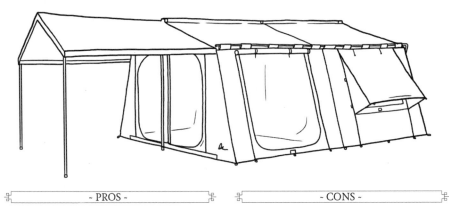

~ PROS ~	~ CONS ~
Strong retro looks – many of these still come in colours like sludgy orange or brown, which is good.	*Can be cumbersome – the older models are heavy to erect.*
They're great for families – small children can be put to bed in their own room. You can use another room for sitting or eating or cooking (be careful).	
Great for rainy countries – because you can, in theory, cook inside, they're also ideal for camping in bad weather.	
Good headroom – I'm 1.8m tall and definitely appreciate this point!	

~ The army tent ~
Best for value

There isn't - strictly speaking - such a thing as an army tent. But a quick trawl of an army surplus warehouse or eBay will throw up lots of solid, simple canvas army-style tents, from a tiny one-man thing to a marquee-style mess tent. We bought two small, green canvas American army ones, which appeared to have been used - though we don't know whether in military operations or not. They cost £4 each on eBay (we actually only meant to buy one, but such is the joy of eBay).

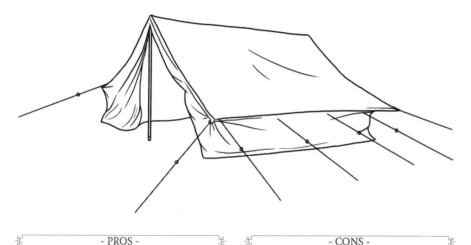

- PROS -	~ CONS ~
They are cheap - often very cheap.	*Big can be tricky - some of the larger ones can be cumbersome to erect and very heavy.*
Simple, stylish good looks - the fact that they are often recycled also means that they generally have a good aged look as soon as you buy them; no one wants to look like a novice.	*The problem with pre-loved - there's always a risk with second-hand tents that some vital bits and pieces (pegs, ropes, that sort of thing) might be missing. So double-check before you head off into the woods.*
They are generally canvas - so good in hot and cold weather.	
Simplicity - they're very easy to erect.	

~ The bell tent ~
Best for weekends away

My first memory of camping is in my dad's camouflage bell tent. I was about six and imagined that Dad had got his tent when he was in the army; it didn't occur to me that he hadn't been in the army. We camped in the woods in Scotland with my cousin and had to go home early because of the midges. We use our own European bell tent several times each year; for now it's our favourite - it looks good and is easy to put up.

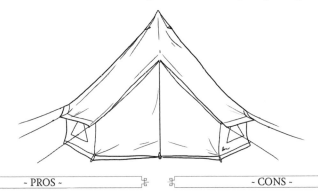

~ PROS ~	~ CONS ~
A design classic. And it's made of canvas, not throwaway nylon.	*They can be pretty heavy - so only pitch one when you can access the camping site with a car or strong wheelbarrow. Do not attempt to carry one on an aeroplane; easyJet wanted us to pay £600 in excess baggage charges for ours. It stayed at the airport.*
All weather - the canvas won't rot and will keep you cool in summer and cosy in winter. The sides roll up for ventilation in hot weather.	
Flexible - groundsheets can be added as required.	
Easy to put up - takes ten minutes maximum.	
Roomy - a good-sized bell tent sleeps up to eight.	

TRAVELLING WITH A TENT

~ JAMES GREENWOOD ~

James Greenwood spent ten years travelling around the world on horseback. He shares his experiences and the lessons he learnt while travel camping which, under no circumstances, should be mistaken for recreational camping – as he explains …

'**I was never looking for relaxing camping.** It wasn't about finding a beautiful spot, it was entirely practical: I needed to get my head down, then get up at first light, pack up and get going again.

'**In the 1200-odd times I camped out, I don't think I ever lit a campfire.** You don't want to upset people by making them think there's some stranger camped at the bottom of their garden – and a fire is the best signal to indicate where you are.

'**In the early days, I'd never take a tent** – they used to be so heavy. If there was nowhere else, I'd sleep under my horse's saddle blankets or, in Romania, under benders - little structures for shepherds made from poles that you throw a tarpaulin over. But they were swarming with ticks. These days there's no excuse not to take a tent. You can now get lightweight bivi tents that weigh less than a kilo.

'**There's nothing worse than setting up camp in the middle of the night and not knowing where you are.** One night, in Turkey, I'd changed plans at the last minute, imagining I'd find somewhere in the next village to stop. When I stumbled upon a timber yard, it seemed – in the dark, at least – a good place to sleep. I woke up to discover I'd settled down in the staff latrine ...

'I couldn't find anywhere to camp in Britain – people weren't that friendly.** One night I spent a particularly cold night in a horsebox.

'It makes me laugh to see people putting in 20 tent pegs,** with guy ropes in every direction. I don't think I've ever put in a tent peg – well, maybe two or three if the wind's really blowing. A high-quality, self-standing lightweight bivouac tent rarely requires pegs or ropes. And even if you're camping alone, go for a two-man – it's so much nicer to have the space.

'Don't waste money on a £50 festival tent** if you're going to be putting it up and taking it down a lot. The most important thing is to use good-quality poles – they should be lightweight with good elasticity and flush joints so you can get them through the guides easily.

'I tended to camp on the wrong side of comfort.** The problem with camping on the right side of comfort is that you carry so much crap and it takes so long to set it all up, use it, and pack it all away again.

'People have a romantic image of camping in barns.** Nice and dry but they're full of rats and mice.

'Always work out where the sun's going to rise.** If you want any kind of lie-in – and the sun hits your tent first thing – forget it. You'll be totally cooked. So pitch your tent in the lee of some early morning shade.

'One of the worst things about camping out is dogs.** If they get any indication that something weird is camped nearby they will bark all night – torture.

'People tend to be polite if they come across you sleeping.** They'd rather avoid a confrontation. One morning, camping on the Afghan/Pakistan border, I was woken by fried eggs, bread and about half a litre of melted butter. Not good for the heart but good for the soul.'

STAYING WARM IN YOUR TENT

When you're camping it is very easy to get cold at night. And being cold at night is not nice. Here are our top tips for keeping cosy.

▶ *Don't skimp on sleeping bags. Get a good warm one, ideally made from natural, breathable fabrics so you are warm but not sweating. (See p.244, 'the best kit for the great outdoors' for our recommendations.)*

▶ *Wear socks in your sleeping bag (but do not wander around outdoors in them; getting them wet before you get into your sleeping bag is not clever). Consider a hat.*

▶ *Pocket handwarmers are good for cold hands (see our 'best kit' guide, p.250, for more information) And if you're very organised, take a hot-water bottle (and a suitable campfire kettle or Kelly Kettle, see p.251, to fill it).*

▶ *It is more important to have a something underneath you than on top as more damp and cold comes from the ground than the air (a Duluth sleeping bag roll – see our 'best kit' guide, p.250 – is very good, or you could use sheepskin or a wool blanket). But ideally you'll have a blanket to pull over you too as well as something under you.*

▶ *Children can fidget their way out of sleeping bags during the night, so rely more heavily on what they're wearing than what they're sleeping in.*

▶ *Wool blankets are best. We like the ones from Early's of Witney (see the 'best kit' guide, p.245, for details) but fleece is good. Two thin blankets are better than one thick one as the air between them adds insulation.*

▶ Wear thin layers of natural fabrics to sleep in. Cashmere or merino long johns and T-shirts are made by many companies that sell thermal underwear. (See the section on p.158, about the evolution of outdoor clothing to read more on this.).

▶ If you can, pitch your tent behind a windbreaker – a building, wall or your car.

▶ Go for a brisk walk or sit by the campfire just before you go to bed, to give you a good head start.

▶ If it's really cold, you could insulate your tent, or the sleeping area inside it, too. If lack of wind and rain allow, blankets and large stones will do the job from the outside. Or attach a rope lengthways over your sleeping area, to the inside of the tent at the top. Drape a large blanket over this to form a 'tent within a tent'. Make sure it is long enough to bunch up on the ground around you and keep drafts out and that it is does not touch the tent itself, as this will let moisture in.

CAMPSITE ETIQUETTE

~ DIXE WILLS ~

You may dream of pitching a tent in the woods ... but find yourself on a campsite. So we asked seasoned site tester, Dixe Wills, author of *Tiny Campsites* – which we love – to give us the low-down on communal camping manners.

~ How to make friends and influence people (or successfully avoid them) on a campsite ~

Shh ...!

Many unwritten campsite rules are probably true in life generally, but sound may be the exception: rib-stock nylon is no barrier. While you think you're talking quietly in your tent, everyone in the field can hear you. And if you're doing more than talking ...

To sing, or not to sing?

Campsites that encourage campfires are often the sorts of places you can get out a guitar and share a tune until one in the morning. But never assume.

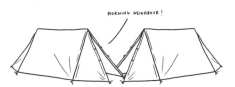

Keep your distance

When you walk into a near-empty railway carriage, you don't sit next to the only occupant, do you? The same rule applies in sparsely populated campsites.

Pet politesse

I've had free-roaming dogs eating my food and poohing beside my tent. Quite unpleasant.

Beware of wafts

You may be proud of your spicy ribs, but your neighbours won't appreciate the smell from your cooking inside their tent. Search for the shelter of a wall or your own pitch.

Put a sock in it

I like to be cheery and say 'hello' but what I dread, and what I suspect a lot of other people dread, is the person who comes over to say 'hi' and goes on and on and on (while perhaps eying your dinner longingly). Do respect others' privacy.

When you've got to go

On sites with no facilities you've got options: a public loo nearby, the pub - or, alternatively, invest in a folding trowel. Burn loo paper in the hole (as far from tents as possible) and cover over. Not the world's greatest experience but you get used to it.

And if all else fails ...

Camping in Britain is usually is a good thing: I've had very few poor experiences, and those have usually been due to the weather. Generally, people are nice: I've been offered a lot of cups of tea.

WHERE'S THE REMOTE ?

Don't get boxed in

The sound of chatting, unless in the middle of the night, is just people having a nice time. But those who bring a television and impose their evening's viewing on the campsite - that annoys me. Why not stay home?

CAMPFIRES AND WOOD

~ CHARLIE ~

'How come it takes a single match to start a forest fire, but a whole box to start a campfire?' **Anon**

~ Building the perfect campfire ~

We love campfires; in many ways they are at the root of much that is best about family life outdoors. Not because we have campfires all of the time - we don't - but because there is no warmer, happier, more unified or complete feeling than lounging round a campfire with our children and friends after a big supper has been devoured and looking at the stars while talking nonsense and sipping on something appropriate.

Fire was the first thing that truly set us apart from other animals; once we could make a good fire we could cook, fend off predators and stay warm.

The essence of a good fire is a reliable method of lighting, good tinder and good wood.

~ Prepare the ground ~

First, scrape a bit of ground clear of dry grass or pine needles or whatever and build a good surround with stones. The more careful you are at this stage, the more you can relax later. We didn't build a good enough surround once when we were on holiday in a very dry France, and nearly lost control of our fire.

~ Create a spark ~

We have tried using things such as flints, like real men, to spark fires and have made them work, but we far prefer something simple like matches, a lighter or even - our favourite - a firesteel (a piece of ribbed steel, along which you drag another piece of metal to create a spark - we sell them at Pedlars). If you are worried about getting matches damp you can buy the expensive all-weather versions (available in most camping shops and which are incredibly efficient) or dip normal matches lightly in varnish, which not only protects them but makes them burn more fiercely, too.

~ Love me tinder ~

The best tinder is probably dry newspaper, which needs to be bundled up, loosely in single sheets to light a good fire. If newspaper isn't available, try tiny dry twigs mixed with equally dry pine needles, unravelled natural rope or shredded cedar or redwood bark. Whatever you use, make sure the tinder is dry. If everything to hand

is wet then the inner wood of a semi-rotten log sometimes works.

~ From small beginnings ~

Next you need lots of kindling. Softwood - wood from conifers/evergreens - makes the best kindling; but most woods will work well if they are small, dry and you have a good quantity (more than you imagine you need). The key is to find bits of dead - but not too rotten - wood; wood torn from living trees damages the tree and has a very high water content. Pile the kindling onto the tinder in a loose conical shape; you need to let air get to the fire, so don't pack it too tightly.

~ Now for the big boys ~

Once the fire is burning, gently add larger logs, trying to keep a rough conical shape. Hardwoods - generally speaking, broad leaf trees - are best at this stage: they will burn longer and hotter than softwoods (see above). You'll always use more wood than you think you'll need.

~ Damp squib ~

Finally, make sure that the fire is properly extinguished before you move on. This may sound a bit elementary but fires can take root and travel underground if the ground is made of peat or a deep mulch of leaves or needles.

~ Prepare for cook off ~

To make your campfire suitable for cooking on the simplest thing is to find some sort of metal grill; sometimes we use a shelf from the oven, but it takes a hell of a lot of scrubbing before it is suitable for use in the oven again. Lay it over the rocks that surround the fire, or drop some stones of a suitable size in to hold it up (do build the fire around the grill rather than the other way around if you do plan to cook on it). The other key thing I'd suggest building in is a tripod from which to hang your kettle and any saucepans; you can also buy these – but if you build your own do it out of solid wood and make sure it's high enough for the flames not to reach it, and that it is outside the stones so it's not sitting in the fire.

Follow the guide below and get an idea of how it should look from the drawing.

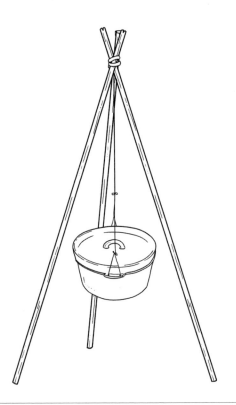

AXES

'People love chopping wood.
In this activity one immediately
sees results.' **Albert Einstein**

~ Swing for it: our family's surprising axe history ~

My great-great-grandfather was four times Prime Minister to Queen Victoria. He was a man of massive physical as well as mental ability. He lived much of his life in cities, but he was a countryman at heart and his absolute love was chopping down trees. It sounds a bit whacky nowadays but his hobby served two purposes. First, there were a lot of trees to be chopped on the family estate, in North Wales, and he was as good a person as any to perform this task. And second - as anyone who has ever tried it will have found out - chopping a tree down is really hard work and will keep you incredibly fit, as indeed he was until late in his life.

William Gladstone became famous for this pastime and he was given axes on hundreds of official visits. We still have them at home. He was a huge celebrity and people - in their hundreds, and often thousands - would come to the woods near to his Welsh home to collect chippings as souvenirs of the trees that he chopped down. There were so many souvenir hunters, in fact, that a system was developed whereby people could collect a chunk of wood only on receipt of a voucher from the PM's office. Strange times.

Still, all of this might partly explain why I think that chopping wood with an axe is such a great thing to do. But lots of people, boys and girls, men and women, love swinging an axe. It's a simple, primeval thing; there is something incredibly exciting and fulfilling about chopping your own logs, even if it is (as in my case) a vaguely gratuitous exercise related to having a campfire. Whatever, there are a few basic rules to follow if you are chopping down a tree:

▶ First, please remember that axes are very dangerous things indeed.

▶ Hold on tight to avoid a flying axe after impact (it's easier to let go than you might think).

▶ Remember that it is the weight of the axe that chops, not the force of the swing.

▶ Swing rhythmically.

▶ Chop at an angle – because if you don't it tends to bounce back more, but at an angle it's easier to get into the wood.

▶ Be really careful, particularly of your feet. Before embarking on your first good chop, it is probably best to get a basic lesson from someone so as not to chop your toes off. And I recommend a pair of steel toecap boots, which can look the business, too.

▶ If an axe is not your thing, then a small saw is a good alternative.

▶ See our 'best kit' guide, p.244, for details of axes we recommend.

> 'Give me six hours to chop down a tree and I will spend the first four sharpening the axe.'
> **Abraham Lincoln**

~ Caring for your axe ~

Despite Abraham Lincoln's notion, above - which is probably intended to have a wider meaning anyway - caring for your axe is relatively simple.

Axes shouldn't be stored in a room without moisture or that is too hot, as this may split the wooden handle. Most axe bits will benefit from occasional oiling and linseed oil is best for this.

If the bit is particularly damaged, you may need to reshape and grind it. Unless you have a grinder, this will probably need to be done by a professional; the key thing is to make sure that you keep the original shape and bevel, as these are integral to the design of the tool.

If the damage is relatively minor, then a file, a whetstone and a couple of clamps to hold the axe in place are all you need. A pair of good, strong leather gloves is a good idea, too.

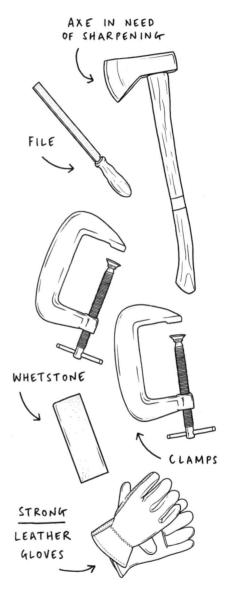

AXE IN NEED
OF SHARPENING

FILE

WHETSTONE

CLAMPS

STRONG
LEATHER
GLOVES

SURVIVAL TIPS

Notes

MIDGES, WASPS, TICKS AND SNAKES

- CAROLINE -

~ Midges ~

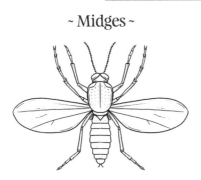

Midges, or 'no see 'ums' as they are also sometimes called, can be the bane of life in the great Scottish outdoors particularly, although they are also found in certain parts of Ireland, Wales and Cornwall. Unlike the usually solitary mosquito, midges hunt in packs. In fact, they hunt in great clouds of minuscule little black beasts that none of the traditional insect repellents seem able to hold at bay. They can ruin an afternoon walk, a barbecue, or a morning in the garden. They swarm indiscriminately and leave their victim covered in tiny red bites, which itch almost more than any mosquito bite, especially behind the ears and the back of the neck.

They appear from early April and hang around until late October. The only weather that keeps them away is a breeze.

No surprise, then, that many have tried to come up with a solution to keep them at bay. One option is the effective but unattractive midge net helmet, usually khaki in colour, it tucks into the collar of your jacket, and is made of nylon with either a very fine mesh or a transparent plastic bit for you to see through. These can be bought in any good outdoor shop, but they can be hot and sweaty on a warm day, and are no good if you are trying to enjoy an evening barbecue.

We have tried citronella and most big-name insect repellents to no or little avail. We even tried something called a Midge Magnet, which proved to be an expensive mistake. The Midge Magnet purported to dispense male midge pheromones into the air, with the aim of attracting the female (biting) midges. When the females were within striking distance, the Magnet sucked them into a very fine mesh bag, a bit like a giant outdoor vacuum cleaner. But it was large and unwieldy, it had to be frequently recharged and only really worked if you were within a 1.8m radius of its humming output. No good for a midge-free walk, or a peaceful afternoon in the garden. The only thing, other than the midge net helmet, that seems to work is smoke – from wood, heather, cigarettes or cigars. But even with those, you literally have to be enveloped in a cloud of smoke to keep the clouds of midges away. Not very healthy or very pleasant.

However, at last, there is a solution: an unlikely but truly effective one. The lovely people at Avon have developed a dry body oil, a very good moisturiser called Skin So Soft, which turned out to have an unexpected quality: it is also a miracle midge and mosquito repellent.

No one seems to know quite how the discovery of the moisturiser's

repelling powers came about, but it is so effective that members of the army and Forestry Commission apparently stock up on it regularly, and any self-respecting gamekeeper or farmer will always have a bottle to hand. It's also sold as a mosquito and midge repellent in several outdoor shops we've been to. It certainly works for us; we all use it and also put it on the horses. It's incredible *and* it smells nice!

~ Wasps ~

Everyone knows how frustrating the battle against wasps can be, and how painful if you irritate them enough that they sting you. 'Why do wasps even exist?' has been the refrain from our children over many a summer. We have had some pretty eccentric solutions suggested to us for keeping them at bay, and we have tried them all …

One friend suggested that if you move your hands alternately, in a fast backwards and forwards motion either side of a wasp, as close as you dare, but certainly about 50-75cm either side of it, then the wasp will be hypnotised and fall down, asleep. We have never been able to make this work, but perhaps we haven't ever perfected the technique.

Another supposed fail-safe solution is to buy some cheap coffee filter papers and some cheap ground coffee, put the filter in a heatproof bowl, fill it with ground coffee, position it near the table and set light to the filter paper. The resulting acrid smoke does indeed keep the wasps at bay, but also drives away all but the most stalwart!

The thing that always works the best is the good old wasp trap; a jar you hang in the garden, filled with a sweet, sticky mixture that first attracts and then catches the insects. You can either buy a beautifully crafted glass wasp trap, or use an old jam jar. The trick is to make the solution you put inside it sweet enough to attract the wasps away from where you are trying to enjoy some home-made jam on toast for breakfast.

Make a solution using jam, fruit juice, honey, sugar, fizzy orange, cordial, anything that comes to hand, and fill the jar half-full. The theory is that the wasps will be so intoxicated by the sweetness that they fall into the solution and drown. Place the trap far enough away from the table so that the wasps are drawn away, about 1.8m, but make sure it is on a wall or a ledge so that no one kicks it over accidentally and gets multiple stings from a sticky mass of dead and dying wasps. (I have learnt the hard way that wasps can still sting you when they're dead!) Empty the trap every few days, but make sure all the wasps are dead before emptying it. The best way is to put the lid back on the jam jar and give it a good shake. Once you are sure they are all dead, empty the sticky contents somewhere safe and far away, and start again.

~ Ticks ~

Ticks are nasty, burrowing, blood-sucking creatures and if you have ever been unfortunate to have one, you will know how unpleasant they are, how itchy and sore their bite site is, and how dirty they leave you feeling. The best thing to do is avoid getting them in the first place, so if you are walking in tall grass or through heather in the spring and summer, wear long boots or gaiters to protect your lower legs.

If you do get a tick, the chances are that you won't notice it until it has sucked enough blood to swell its nasty little body. A tick is a tiny black thing, so small you can barely see its legs: the bit you'll see is its back-end as it burrows its head into your skin to get to your blood. Our parents used to burn them off with cigarettes, but I am not sure that this is recommended nowadays. The best way is to get one fingernail and thumbnail, or a pair of tweezers, as close to the tick's head as possible, and pull gently until it lets go. However, this can risk pulling off the body, but leaving the head inside, which can cause an infection. Another, less effective way, which we always defaulted to as children, is to soak a cotton wool ball in vodka, and saturate the tick until it falls off. The problem is that the tick doesn't always submit to intoxication ...

Although ticks are a nasty irritation if you are a human, they rarely spread diseases (although the tiny Blacklegged Tick does spread Lyme disease, in rare cases). However, ticks do spread diseases in cats, dogs and horses, so it is important to keep these tick-free by checking and removing any that you find, and by tick-treating from April till September with a reliable treatment from the vet. Prevention is always better than the cure.

~ Snakes ~

Adders are the only really venomous snake in the United Kingdom. An adder bite may not kill you if treated properly, but it will leave you feeling drowsy, nauseous and feverish with an almighty bruise and swelling at the bite site. Just after leaving school, some friends and I went on a post A-level camping trip to Boscastle. We'd just got the tent up, a huge 12-man army one, and went for a walk along the clifftop. Suddenly one of my friends felt a pain in her ankle; we thought she'd just smacked her leg on a stick . . . until she got this huge, painful swelling. We carried her back to a farmhouse and realised she'd been bitten by an adder. That was the end of our celebrations: we took her to the hospital and she ended up on crutches for a month.

Although they are not aggressive snakes, adders will attack if they are trodden on or feel under threat. Always wear long boots or gaiters if you are out walking in adder country as the most obvious bite site is the ankle. And never ever poke an adder with a stick. Snakes are most active in the summer months and adders are relatively common in areas of rough, open countryside and often found at the edge of woods. They like to bask in the sun on rocks and near streams. Most adders have a distinctive zigzag stripe down their backs, with an inverted V behind their heads. Males are pale grey or white with a black zigzag, and females are pale brown with a brown zigzag. They are the most frequently seen of the three native British snakes (the others being the harmless grass snake and the rare smooth snake – though the slow-worm is often mistaken for another, but it is in fact a lizard without legs and, again, harmless).

Although no human has died from an adder bite in Britain in the last 20 years, adders can and do kill dogs. We lost our golden retriever Storm to an adder four years ago. She and her best friend, Shadow, were out in the heather on the hill behind our house in Scotland, ferreting about as dogs do, and all I saw was a double flash of something pale in the heather followed by a terrible yowling from both dogs. I knew something awful had happened, so I bundled them straight into the Land Rover and rushed them to the vet. He confirmed that they had both been bitten by an adder and although he gave them both antidotes, Storm died in the night. We think that Shadow had disturbed the sleeping snake and so had only been scratched by the venom-loaded fangs, and by the time Storm came past five seconds later, the snake was wide awake and poised to strike. It was a terrible day for us all, and I still miss Storm even now. The lesson learnt is that vigilance is key to safety.

THE EVOLUTION OF OUTDOOR CLOTHING

~ GRAHAM HOYLAND ~

You'd expect a mountaineer to know a bit about what makes outdoor clothing good. But there can't be many who know quite as much as the climber, Graham Hoyland, relative of 1924 Everest climber Howard Somervell. Somervell had lent George Mallory his camera for the adventurer's bid to reach the great mountain's summit with Andrew Irvine. Mallory and Irvine never returned.

Graham had already been on nine expeditions to Everest, searching for his relative's camera and trying to unravel what happened to Mallory. And not only did he become the 15th Briton to reach the summit – he also led the expedition that discovered Mallory's body, during the filming of a BBC documentary he was making about the fatal trip. It was this which, in part, prompted his return to the mountain for the Mallory Replica Clothing Project, which painstakingly recreated Mallory's climbing outfits. Every piece was remade by hand and put into action by Graham on Everest, as part of his quest to discover what had gone wrong for Mallory . . .

'Someone once said there's no such thing as bad weather, just bad clothes. When I got to base camp for the project, I opened up this great big aluminium flying case and there were Mallory's clothes. The first thing I sensed was a wonderful smell; lovely woollen silk and cotton – natural fibres. The colours were wonderful too, muted pastels, and the feel was soft and welcoming. Completely unlike modern fleeces, which are made out of recycled plastic bags, at best. The naturalness of the fibres was immediately attractive. And to wear it was much more flexible and light than modern bulky down clothing.

'I wanted to see if Mallory and Irvine's clothing had been adequate for them to have got to the summit or not. And in short: yes it was, but only just. On a warm day, one Sherpa famously took all his clothes off on the summit, so that proves that on a good day you could survive up there naked. But the fact is that when it gets cold, and it gets damn cold on Everest, you could die very swiftly in the clothing Mallory was wearing.

Nevertheless, it was far better and more protective than people had assumed.

'An American researcher called Tom Holzel had described Mallory's clothing as a "hacking jacket and a muffler", which was absolute nonsense. The top layer was a polar jacket; the sort of thing Shackleton would have worn. Underneath were seven alternating multilayers of wool, cotton and silk, which slip against each other with very little friction, so you could walk with considerable ease and using less energy walking. So this was actually the very best sort of clothing that they could have had then; it was cutting-edge technology of the time.

'There were some very clever little details, such as an "articulated pivot sleeve", a triangular piece of fabric under the armpits, which Burberry had patented in 1901. Normally when you lift your arm above your head when you're climbing, your shirt tail whips out behind your back and you get a sudden blast of cold air in your kidneys just when you don't want it. But this design stops that.

'Where I live, in the High Peak in Derbyshire, that's another thing altogether. There's no clothing I've found yet that can keep you dry during a wet summer in England. When I go out for a walk across the moor, I don't give my clothing a moment's thought. I just wear whatever is closest – a jumper and a pair of wellies – and I'm often passed by people wearing enough gear to get to the summit of Everest . . . They must look at me and think I'm a complete idiot.

'I'd say the evolution of outdoor clothing has been driven by consumerism. The clothes I tested were very expensive when they were around. I saw how long they took to make, to hand knit the socks – and nowadays outdoor clothes are knocked up in Chinese sweatshops out of petrochemicals. And that's really what I learnt: that the clothes they wore in the past were very expensive, wonderfully handcrafted and had an awful lot more thought to them than we ever suspected. I'd like to start wearing more natural clothes from the past, like tweed jackets, which are warm and work perfectly well in the wet.

I'll probably look a bit of a fogey – but those clothes were far better than we ever thought.'

WILD FOOD

Notes

FORAGING

- JAMES GRAHAM-STEWART -

James Graham-Stewart – or Tall James as he's called by our children, because, well, you can guess why – is an antiques dealer; he really knows his stuff. And so he lives a largely metropolitan life. But at heart, he's one of a rare breed, a true countryman with a deep interest in, and knowledge of the great outdoors. He has taught us all quite a bit about foraging; whenever he visits us we ask him to go and find us something interesting to eat. And he never lets us down. Here is his guide ...

'Finding food in the wild clicks you into a different world. Especially picking mushrooms, when it is the strange world of the forest floor you enter, a world of weird coloured lichens and mosses. But whatever you pick – tiny wild strawberries, lemony sorrel, young, fresh nuts – it gives you a real connection with nature, and it's very satisfying.

'In England, there are rules about public access: in short, you need the landowner's permission to walk on their land (though interestingly not to pick wild-growing food on it – unless you are apprehended in the act when the landowner can ask you to leave, but cannot confiscate your foraged things. Worth knowing!). In Scotland, there is no law of trespass so there you can just go in and pick as you wish. Far more civilised.

'Bear in mind that some cultivated land may have been treated with pesticides – so the wilder, the better.'

* Never eat anything you cannot identify with 100 per cent certainty. Never eat anything decaying – it could indicate weedkiller; be environment-aware – in other words, are there fumes, dogs, etc. nearby? For more information on foraging, type 'foraging dos and don'ts' into the Food Standards Agency search box, at: Food.gov.uk

~ James's favourite forages ~

~ Comon sorrel ~

~ Chickweed ~

You can find this sharp-tasting leaf all over the British Isles; it grows all summer long on old grassland that has been left to its own devices. The trick is to find the stuff that hasn't already been grazed by the sheep. Under bracken is good, as they can't reach to nibble at it there and so it grows stronger and bigger. Sorrel is easy to spot and has a distinctive appearance; where the stem meets the leaf it looks a bit like the ace of spades, and the leaf comes away very steeply.

The taste is lemony; sorrel is quite bitter but very nice and it tastes especially good raw in salads. When it's cooked it becomes a bit more like spinach. Generally, it is a very good flavouring.

Though you may know this plant best as a gardening irritation, chickweed is, in fact, delicious. Again, it is very good raw in a salad, and has a nutty taste.

The little, green creeping plant has small clusters of white flowers and leafy, ground-covering stems; it grows very late in the year and is pretty much everywhere – though it prefers damp, shady environments. You can pick it right into the early winter. Use it as you would use spinach, put it in a salad or make pesto from it.

~ Fat hen ~

~ Hawthorn ~

This is a fairly rampant weed, commonly found on wasteland, roadside verges, hedgerows and gardens. It grows vertically, and to heights of up to 1m; the leaves are a diamond shape.

It tastes good – especially when the leaves are picked young in spring or early summer; it's a good green to steam, and you'll always get lots of it. Use it as you would spinach or chard.

Most hedges in Britain are hawthorn and it is the most common of the hedge plants. The leaves, which grow in clusters from hard, woody stems, taste best picked young, in the early spring, when they will also be a vibrant green. The leaves are very good in salads.

In the autumn, hawthorn berries appear and these are good for making haw jelly (see recipe for rowanberry jelly, p.173: you can adapt the same process to make jelly or jam with any foraged fruit). Pick them in the spring.

~ Wild watercress ~

~ Strawberries ~

This, again, is widespread and grows mainly in freshwater springs. The taste is just like the stuff you buy in the shops, though better, of course, because you've picked it yourself.

You have to be careful with it though, on two counts. Firstly, there's a poisonous plant called hemlock water dropwort that it could be mistaken for by the unwary, so you want to avoid that. Secondly, you have to be careful if it's growing near to grazing land, as there's a parasite you can catch from the animals through the water called liver fluke. So unless you're confident the cress has grown in a spring that no livestock – especially sheep – has access to, steer well clear. If you are in any doubt, cook it and put it in a soup.

There are lots of wild fruits in Britain, and wild strawberries are fairly common. The plant is unmistakable with its broad, ribbed leaves and its tiny white flowers with a yellow centre in spring. They're often escapees from gardens, growing on limestone walls or in woodland, and you pick them in July/August. They're tiny but delicious.

The leaves, steeped in hot water and drunk as a tea, or sprinkled over a salad, are also said to have health-giving properties, but I go straight for the fruit.

~ Wild raspberries ~

These are also widespread and found in hedgerows, on riverbanks and open bits of woodland. The east coast of Scotland is particularly good for them; they do not like too much heat. Pick them throughout the summer and autumn. They are ripe when they come away from the stem easily.

~ Elderflowers ~

These are abundant in hedges in the spring and wonderful for making either elderflower cordial (see p.xx for the recipe) or champagne. Pick them before they become too musty. Choose a dry, sunny day when the flowers are in full bloom.

~ Bilberries ~

Find them on bits of moorland or in birch woodlands; they're very good; similar to blueberries, but smaller. They are sweet and intensely flavoured and make your lips and fingers go purple. They make an excellent crumble, particularly.

Bilberries are laborious to pick, though, as they are so small. There used to be a thing you could get here called a bilberry comb, or scrabbler, which you'd rake through the bush to pull off the fruit. You can still get them in the US where they're called bilberry rakes, though apparently a metal Afro-comb and a clean dustpan make for a decent substitute to speed things up.

~ Damsons ~

~ Hazelnuts ~

The damson – a sort of wild, bitter plum – and delicious, is often overlooked in hedgerows. Damsons make very tart jams (see the recipe for blackberry jam, p.174, though obviously with damsons you'd need to remove the stones).

They are not the most common of the hedgerow fruits; so well done if you spot some. They look a lot like sloes (which are in the same family) but are redder in colour, larger, and an oval shape, rather than round.

A word of warning: the trees often have large thorns, so gardening gloves aren't a bad idea.

As these were one of the few things you could take in the autumn and store all winter, hazelnuts used to be a very important source of protein for country people. If you eat them fresh off the tree, in September/October, they are green and milky and fresh; or you can dry them to save for cooking or just eating as they are.

Dry them in a warm airing cupboard or over a not-too-hot radiator (which only takes a couple of days). Make sure they have a good airflow; on top of a rack on or inside some netting or loose sackcloth would be good.

~ Mushrooms ~

You always have to be careful about identifying things; but it's crucial with mushrooms and water plants (see 'wild watercress', above).

A good mushroom book is essential. Roger Phillips is extremely good (see p.258). And only eat what you are absolutely certain of: they can kill you. I once picked some button field mushrooms and when we came to prepare them, one was a button death cap. The latter, which has distinctive white gills, is indistinguishable from the button field when it is closed. The death cap would kill you; there's no grey area about that, and no antidote.

In France you can take any mushrooms you have gathered into any pharmacy, and they will tell you there and then which are edible and which are not. That can be a little disheartening if you have spent hours gathering a basket of what turns out to be highly toxic fungi, but better safe than sorry!

If you are armed with the facts though, there is nothing better than finding and eating your own mushrooms (see p.206 for recipe). Prime picking season is late summer/autumn until the first hard frosts - good luck!

~ Five Mushrooms ~

~ Chanterelle ~

A distinctive and common fungi, which grows plentifully, so once you find a patch, you'll get lots of them. These proliferate in deciduous woodlands, but not spruce.

~ Hedgehog mushrooms ~

The distinctive thing about these mushrooms, also found in deciduous woodland, is that the underside looks like tripe - it has neither gills nor tubes, but little white spines, thus the name. Has a good meaty texture and very substantial, not unlike the cep.

~ Ceps ~

The best of all mushrooms is the cep, or, in Italian, the porcini or, in English, the penny bun. It is part of the boletus family, which, most commonly, grows in deciduous woodland.

Ceps can be difficult to spot because they are so well camouflaged. They have a distinctive spreading tree-trunk-like stem and the cap varies widely in colour from a pale buff to dark brown and has a dry-textured, rather than slippery cap.

Instead of the gills you usually see on the undersides of mushrooms, the boletus family has tiny tubes. There's only one poisonous member of that family, called 'Satan's boletus' which is red, so you're reasonably safe.

~ Giant puffball ~

These white ball-shaped mushrooms can be anything up to the size of a football. They grow in old pasture, i.e., open grassland that hasn't been cultivated for a long time. To eat these strange-looking things, cut them into 2.5cm 'steaks'. The trouble with a puffball is it soaks up as much butter or oil as you throw at it, because of its spongy texture. I like to treat them as I would French toast; dip them into seasoned, beaten egg to seal before frying in a little oil or butter with garlic and parsley.

~ Lawyers' wigs ~

These also grow on old pasture; though outside my office, which is in an old London gasworks, there are half a dozen sprouting through the asphalt. But they're more common in gardens or any short grassland.

Tall and elegant, they are very upright with an elongated cap; they look like a lawyer's wig, hence the name. These are delicate, not beefy as the cep or hedgehog, and they taste good simply fried with butter, garlic and parsley.

JELLIES, JAMS, PICKLES AND CORDIAL

~ CAROLINE ~

There can be few things more fulfilling than making something delicious from what you have picked in the hedgerow. All you need to do is add sugar ...

If you've never made jam before, don't be put off by terms like jar sterilisation, sugar thermometers or pectin. Your jars just need to be clean and warmed in a low oven, the set of your jam can be tested on a cold plate and, nowadays, if you buy jam sugar, it has pectin already added. It really is beguilingly simple; jam and jelly making is a wonderfully inexact science.

Read more about foraging for wild food on p.164.

ROWANBERRY JELLY

Rowanberries are the fruit of the rowan, or mountain ash. They are a gorgeous bright orangey-red colour, and appear on the trees in mid to late autumn.

You will need:
Rowanberries
Crab or cooking apples
  (half the quantity to your rowanberries)
Preserving sugar, or jam sugar
  (which has added pectin)
Equipment:
A slope-sided jam pan or heavy-bottomed pan
A jelly bag or muslin square
Sealable jam jars

Pick a basket of ripe rowanberries, remove the stalks, wash and weigh them. For every 450g of rowanberries, allow 225g of crab or cooking apples. Peel, core and dice the apples, put all the fruit into a slope-sided jam pan, or a heavy-bottomed pan, and just cover with cold water. Bring to the boil and simmer until the fruit is soft, about 20 minutes.

Strain the fruit though a jelly bag, or muslin square, into a large bowl. Let it slowly drip through overnight, to get the last precious drops, and don't force it. You can now throw the fruit pulp away.

Measure the juice and allow 450g of sugar for every half a litre of juice. Put the juice and sugar back into the clean heavy-bottomed pan and bring to the boil. Stir until the sugar has dissolved and simmer for about 5 minutes, stirring occasionally. Test for the setting point: drip a drop of the liquid onto a cold plate and if it doesn't run when you tip the plate, it is ready.

Skim off any scum, and carefully pour the liquid into warm, clean jars (to prepare mine, I rinse them out with boiling water and then put them to dry for half an hour on a baking tray in a very low oven). The jelly will keep for ages. Once opened, keep in the fridge.

BLACKBERRY JAM

The problem with picking blackberries for jam is making sure that you don't eat them all on the way.

You will need:
Blackberries
Preserving or jam sugar (the same
weight as the prepared blackberries)
1 lemon per 450g of berries (the lemon
juice here acts as a setting agent)
Equipment:
A slope-sided jam pan or heavy-bottomed pan
Sealable jam jars

Remove any stalks from your blackberries and wash them, if you consider that absolutely necessary. I never do, I just shake them for insects, as boiling the fruit will kill any lurking bacteria. Weigh them and put them into your jam pan (or heavy-bottomed pan), then add the same weight of the sugar (so if you have 450g of blackberries, add 450g of sugar). If you use jam sugar, you don't need to worry about the pectin content of the blackberries and the lemon juice that you add later will give a bit of sharpness to the sweet jam. If you are using ordinary preserving sugar, the acidity of the lemon juice will help the jam set. I'm not sure of the science, but it works!

Stir the sugar into the fruit and leave to stand for about half an hour. This gets the juice running. Transfer the pan to a low heat, add the juice of one lemon and stir until the sugar has dissolved. Turn up the heat and bring the mixture to a rolling boil. Boil for 5 minutes and then drip a couple of drops onto a cold plate to test for the set. If the drop holds its shape when you tip the plate, it is ready. If not, boil for a few more minutes and test again.

Pour the jam into warm, clean jars (see the rowanberry jelly recipe, above, for how I prepare the jars), either straight from the pan, or decanting it into a jug first. Seal the jars immediately and leave to cool.

Again, as with the other recipes, this jam lasts for ages in a cool, dry place.

ELDERFLOWER CORDIAL

This is something else that is deceptively simple to make and it tastes divine, especially with cold, fizzy water and a sprig of mint on a really hot day.

You will need:
20 elderflower heads
1.8kg granulated or caster sugar
About 1.2 litres water
2 unwaxed lemons
60g citric acid
(available from chemist shops or online stockists)
Equipment:
A sieve
A muslin cloth
Sealable glass bottles

Shake out the elderflower heads to get rid of any insects and then put them in a large bowl. Give them a rinse, too, if you like – though I never bother.

Put the sugar into a large pan, add the water, bring to the boil and continue to boil, stirring occasionally, until the sugar has dissolved.

While the sugar syrup is heating, wash the lemons and pare off the rind in quite thick strips with a peeler. Put these in the bowl with the flower heads. Slice the lemons, discarding the top and bottom slices, and add these to the bowl too, giving it all a good toss.

Once all the sugar has dissolved, pour the boiling syrup over the flower heads and lemons and stir in the citric acid. Cover with a clean tea towel and leave for 24 hours.

The next day, strain the cordial through a sieve lined with a muslin cloth, and pour it into clean, dry glass bottles that you've rinsed with boiling water (you can use plastic ones but glass ones look nicer). Seal and put the bottles into the fridge or cupboard, ready to be used. Stored in a cool, dry place, this cordial will last for ages.

PICKLED WALNUTS

Pickled walnuts are excellent with strong cheese and cold meats. The process is long, but so easy, and the resulting pickled walnuts will last for years. Pick the walnuts in May, when the shell is bright green and shiny and the hard shell has not yet formed.

You will need:
2kg walnuts
About 450g salt
For the pickling syrup:
1 litre malt vinegar
500g brown sugar
1 teaspoon ground allspice
1 teaspoon ground cloves
½ teaspoon ground cinnamon
1 tablespoon grated fresh ginger
Equipment:
Sealable jam jars

Pick a bucketful, or 2kg of walnuts (shop-bought walnuts generally won't work, even if you find unshelled ones, as the nuts need to be young).

Wearing rubber gloves, prick each one with a fork a couple of times. The clear juice that will come out as you do this will quickly stain your fingers dark brown, so gloves are a must.

Cover the walnuts with water and stir in about 225g salt. Leave for a week, then drain and start again with a new brine solution. Leave for another week and then drain again. Lay the walnuts on trays in a single layer in a cool, dry, airy place and in a couple of days they will have turned jet black. They are now ready for pickling.

Make the sweet pickling syrup by stirring together all the ingredients in a large saucepan. Bring the mixture to the boil, add the walnuts and simmer for about 15 minutes. The smell will be amazing.

Once the pan contents are cool, fish out the walnuts and spoon them into warm, clean jars (see the rowanberry jelly recipe, above, for method), leaving enough space for the pickling syrup, then cover with the syrup. Seal immediately. These will keep for years.

PLUCKING AND GUTTING A BIRD

~ CHARLIE ~

Plucking a bird is quite laborious and requires patience, but it's hugely satisfying too. And, in many ways, it is a lot more honourable to kill and pluck your own dinner than to buy, say, a pre-plucked chicken from a supermarket that has been killed and plucked in conditions that ... Well, let's not even go there.

A pheasant is probably the largest bird you're likely to pluck but the method, regardless of size, remains the same, though it is harder with certain birds. Ducks and geese, for example, are much tougher work. If you follow the instructions below, you'll be able to pluck pretty much any bird.

There are two conventional methods: wet plucking and dry plucking. The former involves dipping the feathered bird into water that is just below simmering point three times, for about 30 seconds a time, with 30-second breaks in between. Hold the bird by its feet, wearing oven gloves to avoid scalding, and dip it in. This is good if you do not have the time or inclination to hang the bird (though hanging for a few days is always a good idea, as the meat will taste better). Thereafter follow the method for dry plucking, which we prefer because it is more efficient.

~ You will need ~

Some outdoor space (plucking inside
  can make a huge mess)
A bin liner or bucket
Some game/kitchen shears or
  a big knife and chopping board

~ How to do it ~

1. If you can, hang the bird for four to five days. This tenderises the meat and improves its taste. It also makes it easier to pluck. You can freeze the bird before plucking it, if you're short on time; but you are really just postponing the inevitable and, also, making the job of plucking harder. A freshly hung bird is also the easiest to pluck.

2. Start with the tail feathers, pulling these out in ones or twos. (If you are wet plucking and have only a medium-sized pan, you might want to do this before you dip the bird in the water, as you would with dry plucking.) A quick precise yank will do the job. Remember, this is called plucking, not pulling. Then move on to the wings, neck and back. There isn't a great deal of meat on a pheasant wing, so I sometimes just cut the feathered wings off with game shears. Pull the feathers up, one or two at a time, plucking in the direction of growth; they will come away easily. Don't be impatient and pull big clumps out in one go; the skin is quite delicate and you want to leave it intact for cooking. (Where the skin is damaged you can cover the meat with bacon while cooking.) The hardest part is around any gunshot wound or damaged skin; here you'll need to accept that there will be an element of damage but prevent much more by holding the skin in place with the fingers of the hand that isn't plucking the feathers.

3. When the back and neck are reasonably clear of feathers, roll the bird over and start on the breast. Do a good rough job first. There will always be the odd, stubby, stubborn feather left, so pull these out one at a time, once you have got rid of the majority. If there are any left after this you can singe them off with a lighter for a cleaner finish.

4. Chop off the legs where the meat ends, and the head at the base of the neck. This is easy with a good pair of shears or a heavy, sharp knife.

5. *Next remove the crop (the sac in the bird's gullet where it stores half-digested food) and gut the bird. This is easy and very quick. For the crop, insert your fingers into the wound at the neck. You'll soon locate whatever the bird ate just before it died. Pull this out. To gut, place the bird on its back, make a small insertion with the shears, starting at the bottom opening and cutting up towards the breast for about 2cm (or more, depending on the size of the bird; for, say, a goose you'd need to make a larger cut). Put a couple of fingers inside and the innards are easily located; grab hold of them and pull. You can keep the livers for making pâté or whatever.*

6. *Finally, clean the bird under a running cold tap. Pat it dry with kitchen paper and, hey presto, it is ready to cook. You can keep it in the fridge for a few days after this point; some people think that this helps to age it.*

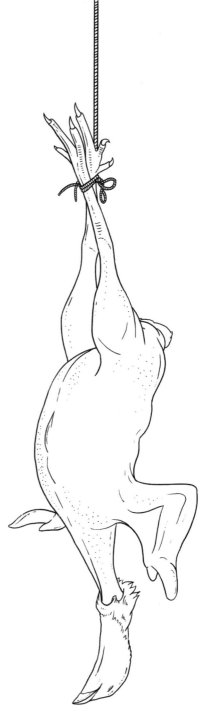

~ Skinning a pheasant ~

This takes much less time than plucking and is an ideal method if you are short of time or if you don't plan to roast the bird and therefore don't need the fatty benefit of the skin. If you do plan to roast your pheasant you can still skin it and compensate with lots of bacon when roasting. It also has the added advantage of not being nearly as messy a process as plucking.

~ How to do it ~

1. Chop the head, wings and legs off as you would when plucking (see above).

2. Remove the tail feathers.

3. Now, roll the pheasant onto its back and pinch some of the breast skin between your fingers. You'll find that it comes away from the flesh easily.

4. Make an incision with a sharp knife and then peel the skin off; the process is similar to taking a coat off the bird, so imagine yourself doing that. You'll find this part of the process surprisingly easy.

5. Finally, clean the crop, gut the bird and clean the flesh as outlined in 'plucking and gutting a bird', above.

~ Hanging game ~

All game benefits from a few days' hanging, to allow the meat to rest and then mature. Four or five days in 55 degrees seems about right for a pheasant to me, although I know that some people believe that a month is ideal. Trial and error will probably teach you how you like your birds.

RIVER FISHING, TROUT TICKLING AND FISH GUTTING

~ CHARLIE ~

'With my silken line
 and delicate hook
I wander in a myriad of ripples
And find freedom.' **Liu Yu**

~ Catching trout with a worm in a river ~

This isn't a guide to fishing, not least of all because I am not a very good fisherman. But as a child I loved fishing for brown and sea trout with a worm; this was, I think, when I was happiest and most at one with nature. Our parents never seemed to worry that we might fall into the river and drown; and they were gloriously unconcerned about whether we'd be home in time for lunch.

So - come rain or shine - entire days were spent dangling worms into the river, and often with spectacular results. And although fishing with worms is not regarded as graceful or sophisticated as fly fishing, there is real skill to it.

All you need is a simple rod, a fishing line and a hook. You can try to make your own out of bamboo, though we tried that a few times and it never worked.

~ How to do it ~

1. First, find your worms. Lift a big stone or stick a spade in the ground near a compost heap and the earth is usually teeming with them. Sometimes you have to root around a bit. Anyway, get more than you think you need and put them into a jar with a pierced lid.

2. When you have decided where to cast your line (see below), thread the worm onto the hook. Do not choose a hook that is bigger than you need, because this means you won't catch small fish (which often taste best of all when fried over a campfire, particularly for breakfast). Size-wise, try a 10 - they go up to around 26 and the larger the number, the smaller the hook; though they do vary brand to brand. For best results, have a chat with the person in the shop you buy it from, as it can be a little complicated at first.

3. If the worm is too big for the hook, cut it in half. Hold the worm by one end and pierce it with the hook's point, then move it over the barb and up the shank. Repeat this in three or four places along the worm's length, covering as much of the hook as possible. You want to have a bit of worm wiggling free of the hook in order to entice fish, but not so much that they can nibble at the bait without getting hooked.

4. Next you need to find a spot where fish are likely to linger. This is where the real skill comes in; and practice makes perfect. As a rule – and I am talking river fishing here – trout like to rest under shady banks. Study the river and you will learn each time you catch one. Move slowly and keep your head down, particularly if it is sunny and make sure any spectators stay well back; fish are very aware of movement and noise. Keep back from the bank by half a metre or so; drop your worm in and try to make sure that it rests above the bed of

the river. You will generally find that if you are going to catch something in this way it will happen in the first few minutes. So, if you don't have any luck, move to another spot.

To find out where in Britain you can catch fish, and to obtain a rod licence (which it is illegal not to have when fishing) go to the Environment Agency's website and type 'where to go fishing' into the search box. *Environment-agency.gov.uk*

~ Tickling trout ~

My dad, his brothers and my godfather – a truly brilliant fisherman – used to pass whole days tickling when they were boys. They taught me how to do it, and made it look quite easy; but I only had success once.

Tickling, or rubbing the belly of a trout until it becomes hypnotised and, therefore, easy to catch seems wildly improbable, but it does work. (Apparently it also works on salmon and eels, though I have never tried either.) And even if you don't succeed, it's still fun grubbing about on a riverbank with your stomach in the grass and your hands in the water.

It's easiest on a small, shallow stream; one where the water is clear and you can see the bottom of the stream and the fish that occupy it. As you pass along the bank, the trout sense you and dart for cover. Your prey are those that head under the bank.

Stay still, watch and figure out where the fish are hiding. Moving slowly, drop down onto the bank and gently put your hands into the water. Assuming you have figured out where the trout is with some accuracy, position your arms under the bank, about half a metre either side of the fish. Move your hands together in a pincer movement, slowly, and making a tickling motion with your fingers. This is not for the squeamish.

When you touch the fish, keep on tickling, gently; perhaps caressing is a better word. The fish will be mesmerised by this and will stay where it is. Now plan your attack. Suddenly and with real commitment and firmness, you are going to have to grab your fish and chuck it as far as possible onto the bank. I am told that grabbing it near to the gills is best but this implies a level of skill that I have never acquired. Do not try to get up; fish are slippery things and in so doing you'll probably mess things up. Just try to grab it and lob it. Once it's on the bank you can give it a mercy blow to the head. You will never, ever eat a more satisfying brown trout.

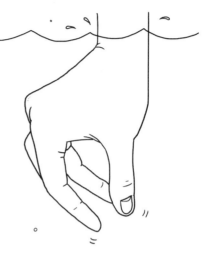

Contrary to some opinions, trout tickling is not illegal. In fact, you don't even need a licence to do it, as fishing licences are for rods. However, there are a few rules about getting into rivers (which you can read about at: *Environment-agency.gov.uk*) and, in England and Wales, you would also need permission from whoever owns the riverbank in question.

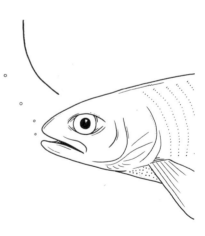

~ Killing a fish ~

This is best achieved with a few smart smacks over the head. If the fish is small enough, hold it and whack it against a rock. If it is bigger, you can hit it with a stick or a priest; a blunt wood and metal object specifically designed for this purpose is called a priest precisely because it is – like a man of the cloth – there at the last moment. You can find one in any fishing shop.

~ Gutting a fish ~

After catching our very first fish when we were young we were taught how to gut it. Inevitably, the bigger the fish, the longer it takes but a reasonable-sized 450g trout should only take a couple of minutes.

~ How to do it ~

Spread out some newspaper if you are doing this indoors, so that you can work over it without causing too much mess. Hold the fish upside down on a flat surface – belly facing you, head away from you – with one hand.

1. Insert a good sharp knife into the bottom opening and cut right up to the head. Be careful not to cut too deeply as you want to avoid piercing the entrails.

2. Spread the two sides of the body cavity apart and then yank out all of the entrails. Depending on the size of the fish, you might need to cut the guts away at the head end. On a smaller fish a good tug will remove them.

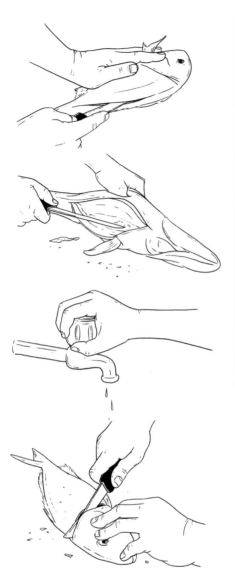

3. *Next, look inside the fish and you will probably see a thin, vein-like membrane at the bottom of the body cavity, running the length of backbone. Run your fingernail or knife along this and you will reveal dark, thick blood. Run the insides of the fish under a powerful cold tap, or in a bucket of river water or just in the river itself to rinse out the inside of the fish thoroughly. Then rinse the outside of the fish clean and you're done.*

4. *If you wish, remove the head with a sharp knife or kitchen shears, but we never do.*

For our favourite outdoor-cooked fish recipes, see p.215.

HOW TO SKIN AND GUT A RABBIT

~ CHARLIE ~

As teenagers we used to borrow a boat and go camping with our cousins on an island in a vast lake in Scotland. We'd take an industrial quantity of beer (our parents didn't know about this bit, I don't think) and the trip generally degenerated into mild chaos. My cousin Roger was a true countryman and he taught me how to gut, skin and spit-roast a rabbit. We'd stalk the rabbits with his air rifle and try and pick off the younger ones – we discovered that the older ones were hard to skin and tough to chew.

~ Gutting it ~

If the rabbit is freshly killed, allow it to cool before you get stuck in. First, push all of the urine from the animal; if you puncture a full bladder the urine will contaminate the meat. Hold the rabbit on a flat surface with one hand, belly up and with its back legs flopping to one side. Apply pressure to the abdomen, and the urine – if there is any – will be expelled.

For the gutting itself, you can do it on any surface but a plastic bag or sack spread across a table or the ground is probably best. Keep the rabbit upside down – i.e., on its back, belly facing upwards, towards you – and hold it with one hand. Make a small incision with a sharp-pointed knife just below the abdomen. Be careful that the knife doesn't go too deep; you don't want to puncture the guts. Cut a hole just big enough to fit two fingers. Insert your fingers and rip open the skin before gently pulling on the guts, but don't try to pull them out. Instead, turn the rabbit the other way up, with its front paws on the plastic sack, and – holding the back legs so that the rabbit is slightly arched – shake it gently over the plastic so that the guts hang out. Now you will be able to remove them: the back end of the guts should pull away easily (take care to remove any droppings) but you will probably need a knife to cut away the innards at the front end (inside the chest), which are harder and drier. To tackle this front end, look inside the cavity, where you should see a thin, transparent membrane. Puncture this with your fingers and pull out the bits – the heart and lungs – inside. Done!

~ Skinning it ~

To skin the rabbit, place it upside down with the head facing you on the plastic. Essentially, you have to unpeel the rabbit by pulling the skin away from the flesh, starting from the hole you made to gut it. If the rabbit is young the skin will come away easily. Of course, it will still be attached to the legs and head and you need to cut these off; a sharp knife is good but strong kitchen scissors are best (having said this, we used to achieve it with the trusty Swiss army knife). To remove the legs, cut them at the knee joints (the sharper and better the knife or scissors, the less likely you are to get nasty splinters of bone). To remove the head, cut

round the neck and then twist apart the vertebrae.

Now wash thoroughly, taking particular care with the insides; and clean the carcass to remove any stray bits of fluff.

To cook, push a sharpened stick through the body of the prepared rabbit and roast it on a patched-together wooden spit. It tastes wonderful.

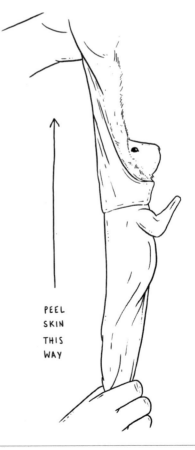

PEEL
SKIN
THIS
WAY

COOKING AND EATING

Notes

HAVE FIRE, WILL COOK

~ CAROLINE ~

Our ideal day in the height of the summer ends with the building of a campfire, knowing that something delicious is going to be cooked over it. In fact our ideal day anytime would end with the building of a campfire, if truth be told. There is something quite intoxicating about the smell of wood smoke.

Some of us are experts in the art of campfire building, and some of us are better at the cooking side of things, and so generally the jobs define themselves rather happily: Charlie is in charge of the fire building and maintenance (see p.144), and I am in charge of the culinary organisation. Eating together as a family is something that we have always tried to do, especially during the holidays when everything is easier and more relaxed. Gathering together round the campfire is the ultimate eating-together experience for us as it combines all our favourite things: family, the outdoors, fires, cooking, fun and laughter.

There are many dos and don'ts that I have learnt along the way, and even now, after many years of outdoor cooking experience, I certainly don't claim to get it right every time. But here are a few tips and techniques that I've tried and tested, to help set you on the right track.

OUTDOOR COOKING TECHNIQUES

~ CAROLINE ~

~ Pit cooking ~

~ How to do it ~

There is a certain caveman/hunter-gatherer romance to pit cooking; basically a hole in the ground in which you bury the food to be cooked, surrounded by hot rocks. It requires hard work and application but, once that is done, there is plenty of time for relaxing and the inevitable bottles of cold beer while the meat cooks. But be warned – it is not a fail-safe method, and it is probably best to avoid cooking chicken or pork this way as it may still be rare after several hours. Better to cook beef or lamb so that, even if this happens, you will not go hungry, and your efforts won't be left unrewarded. And the result, if it works, is tender and delicious and unlike anything you will have tasted before; with the same flavour that you get from slow-roasting, but smokier and earthier.

1. *Dig a rectangular hole about 0.5m deep, 0.5m across and 1m long. Find enough large flatish rocks to line the inside of your pit. The idea is that the pit – once lined with rocks – will be just big enough to hold your meat. Make a neat pile of earth beside your pit; you'll need the soil later.*

2. *Lay and light a large fire in the pit, adding to it until it is really roaring (see 'building the perfect campfire', p.144). Then allow it to burn down, breaking up any large sticks (with a spade or similar) until there is almost nothing left of the fire. This might take an hour or more.*

3. *Meanwhile, prepare the meat. Rub a large leg or a rolled sirloin with olive oil, sea salt and black pepper. Then make small slits all over the meat and stick in slivers of garlic and rosemary leaves. Whatever your choice of meat, wrap it in several layers of foil, making sure it is totally sealed. Originally, banana leaves were used for this, but they are quite hard to get hold of in Europe.*

4. *Once the fire has burned down, the stones that line the pit will be really hot and it will act as your oven. Scoop the remaining hot embers out of the pit with a spade; it is the stones and not the embers that will do the cooking. Drop the meat into the pit. Then cover the pit with some planks and pile all of the soil you dug out on top; this will help to keep the oven warm. Leave it to cook for about 3 hours. Remember, you cannot check the progress, so you must have faith.*

5. *When you dare, cross your fingers, carefully remove the planks and use a spade to remove the soil and stones covering the meat. It should be very hot, so use some oven gloves to unwrap it, then slice it and enjoy!*

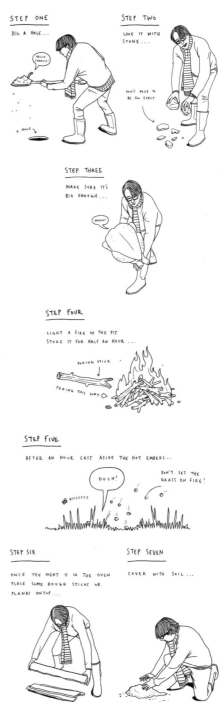

STEP ONE
DIG A HOLE...
HELLO CHARLIE!
A HOLE

STEP TWO
LINE IT WITH STONE...
DON'T NEED TO BE TOO EXACT

STEP THREE
MAKE SURE IT'S BIG ENOUGH...
GREEPY!

STEP FOUR
LIGHT A FIRE IN THE PIT STOKE IT FOR HALF AN HOUR...
POKING STICK
POKING THIS WAY

STEP FIVE
AFTER AN HOUR CAST ASIDE THE HOT EMBERS...
OUCH!
DON'T SET THE GRASS ON FIRE!
BZZZZZZ

STEP SIX
ONCE THE MEAT IS IN THE OVEN PLACE SOME ROUGH STICKS OR PLANKS ONTOP...

STEP SEVEN
COVER WITH SOIL...

~ Mud baking ~

This is probably the messiest but tastiest way of cooking potatoes. You get the smoky flavour, of course, but there is something about getting filthy dirty along the way, and simply eating something cooked outdoors rather than in the oven, seems to make everything taste better.

~ How to do it ~

All you need are the hot embers of a campfire, a bucket of mud and some willing hands. Cover the potatoes in a good coating of cakey-textured mud and drop them carefully into the hot embers. Leave them well alone for about an hour, then fish them out carefully – we use a spade or long tongs for this. Drop them on the ground and the by now hard mud crust will break off. Mash them with lots of butter, salt and pepper, skins and all, and you will rarely have tasted anything so good.

~ Grass steaming fish ~

This is much less difficult than it sounds, and as long as you are sure to really dampen the grass, the likelihood of it catching fire is minimal. You just need to make sure you have a bucket of water at the ready, just in case. Use bigger whole fish: salmon, sea trout, trout or sea bass all work well.

~ How to do it ~

With a sharp knife, cut several armfuls of long grass, whichever sort is to hand. Lay a layer about 1cm thick across your grill, away from the fire at this stage, and throw water across it to damp it down. Put your prepared fish on the grass and cover with a similarly thick layer of grass. Dampen that down too, and then move the grill to the fire. Cook for about 20 minutes, depending on the size of your fish, keeping the grass damp to create the steam. The result is wonderfully light, succulent fish with a hint of wood-smoke. See p.217 for recipe.

~ Baking fish in a newspaper ~

The principle here is the same as grass steaming in that you cook the fish over the fire, but protect it from the naked flames. It also has echoes of good old-fashioned, newspaper-wrapped fish and chips, of course. This method works well for any smallish, firm-fleshed fish. Our favourites are trout and gilthead bream, but the choice is a very personal one.

~ How to do it ~

Take your newspaper and wet each sheet separately; simply splashing water on with your hands is fine. It is important to do it like this, although it is more labour-intensive, otherwise you end up with a soggy mass. Once you have six or so sheets layered up, wrap your fish tightly in the newspaper. If you are doing one big fish, you may want to use more layers, but half a dozen or so should be enough for a fish for two. Put the newspaper bundles onto the grill over the fire and cook for about 20-30 minutes, depending on the size of your fish, turning it halfway through the cooking time and occasionally sprinkling the parcels with water.

When the fish is ready, unwrap it and most of the skin should come off with the newspaper, leaving you to enjoy the delicious, slightly smoky fish, which maybe, just maybe, you have been lucky enough to catch too. (Read about catching and gutting fish on pp.182-7.) And the bonus is that you can burn the newspaper on the fire afterwards, leaving you with minimal rubbish to clear up.

See p.216 for recipe.

~ One-pot cooking ~

This method is ideal for stews, such as the chorizo, red pepper, tomato and butter bean stew (see p.213).

~ How to do it ~

All you really need is a sturdy, flameproof casserole dish and either a trivet to rest it on over the fire, or ideally a tripod on which to hang it over the fire (see 'building the perfect campfire' on p.144). The advantage of the tripod is that you can adjust the height of the casserole dish, so that once you have added all the ingredients, and got your stew going, you can raise it up a little and let it bubble away undisturbed until you are ready to eat.

~ The Essentials ~

~ Be prepared ~

Make sure you have all the right equipment with you before you start – pots, frying pans, spatulas, wooden spoons, sharp knives, olive oil, salt and pepper, whatever you need for preparation and cooking. Over the years, I have bought many classic French baskets and I use those to carry everything I need down to the campfire. But remember that simplicity is the keyword, and to overcomplicate everything takes away from the joy of cooking outdoors.

~ Put a dampener on it ~

Always make sure you have a bottle or jug of water to hand, either to damp down the fire, or for steaming, or to chuck on the fire if it all goes belly-up.

~ Bin there ~

Remember to bring bags or baskets for rubbish that can't be burnt.

MEATY OR FISHY KEBABS AND SKEWERS

Spicy Fish Kebabs, p.203

THE TASTIEST CHICKEN KEBABS

This is a family favourite when something slightly different is required.

Serves 6
You will need:
6 free-range chicken breasts, preferably organic
4 courgettes
For the marinade:
A handful of fresh coriander
A handful of fresh mint
3 fat garlic cloves
6 spring onions
1 red chilli
Zest and juice of 1 lemon
Sea salt and freshly ground black pepper
A little olive oil
Campfire Essentials:
Bamboo skewers pre-soaked for half an hour in water or sticks of fresh rosemary, lower leaves removed, tips kept on

Blanch the courgette discs in salted boiling water for 30 seconds, drain and allow to cool.

Cut the chicken into 2.5cm cubes and place in a ziplock bag. Chop all the marinade ingredients (except the olive oil) very finely, or if preparing this at home, blitz together in a food processor, then loosen to a paste with a little olive oil. Add the marinade to the chicken pieces and mix well, making sure the bag is well sealed. Let the chicken marinate in the fridge or a cool box for at least an hour or longer.

When you're ready to cook, thread alternate pieces of chicken and courgette onto the skewers or rosemary sprigs. Grill for about 5 minutes a side on the hottest part of the fire or barbecue, turning them regularly, until the chicken is cooked through (check by cutting a piece open; if the juices run clear, the chicken is cooked).

CHICKEN KEBABS WITH SATAY SAUCE

This sounds like a very grown-up dish but our children and any young visitors have always pounced on them – probably because the kebabs are easy to pick up and children like that sort of thing. Prepare to make more than you think will be required – they are very popular.

Serves 6
You will need:
6 free-range chicken breasts, preferably organic
For the marinade:
2 teaspoons grated fresh ginger
Juice of 2 limes
Sea salt and freshly ground black pepper
A little olive oil
For the satay sauce:
4-6 tablespoons sesame oil
1 small onion, finely chopped
2 fat garlic cloves, crushed to a paste
  with a pinch of salt
1 small red chilli, chopped
A pinch of chilli powder
1 teaspoon soft brown sugar
1 tablespoon soy sauce or tamari
425ml water
4 tablespoons smooth peanut butter
Juice of 1 lemon
Sea salt
Campfire Essentials:
Bamboo skewers pre-soaked for half an hour in water
  or sticks of fresh rosemary, as before

Prepare the chicken and marinade as in the previous recipe.

For the satay sauce, heat the oil in a pan, add the onion and garlic, and cook until the onion is soft. Add the chopped chilli, chilli powder, sugar, soy sauce (or tamari) and water. Bring to the boil, then stir in the peanut butter and simmer until the sauce has thickened a bit. Add lemon juice and season to taste. Serve cold, or warm in a pan over the fire while the chicken is cooking.

Thread the chicken onto the skewers and grill for about 5 minutes a side, turning regularly, until the chicken is cooked through (cut a piece open to check if the juices run clear). Serve with the satay sauce on the side, or drizzled over the chicken.

LAMB KEBABS

The smoky, spicy marinade takes these into a league above classic lamb kebabs – with a hint of the exotic.

Serves 6
You will need:
500g lamb, trimmed and cut into 2.5cm cubes
2 red peppers, deseeded and cut into 2.5cm pieces
For the marinade:
1 tablespoon smoked paprika
2 cloves
½ teaspoon cumin seeds, or ground cumin
2 teaspoons coriander seeds or ground coriander
Sea salt and freshly ground black pepper
Olive oil
Campfire Essentials:
Bamboo skewers pre-soaked for half an hour in water
*   or sticks of fresh rosemary, as before*

First bash up all the spices for the marinade in a pestle and mortar until fine, then mix with enough olive oil to make a thick marinade paste.

Put the lamb pieces and marinade into a ziplock bag, close and shake to cover well. Leave somewhere cool for half an hour to an hour.

Then, using the skewers or rosemary sprigs, spike each piece of meat alternately with the peppers. Grill for around 5 minutes, turning them regularly, to give you nicely charred meat on the outside and juicily pink on the inside.

SPICY FISH KEBABS

Kebabs are usually associated with red meat or chicken, but fish works brilliantly as well – you can use any sort of fish, just make sure it has firm flesh that won't crumble.

Serves 6

You will need:

500g monkfish tail
  (or cod or haddock or similar firm-fleshed fish),
  trimmed of all skin and bone and cut into
  2.5cm cubes
255g boiled new potatoes, halved

For the sauce:

2 thumb-sized pieces fresh ginger, thinly sliced
Juice and zest of 1 lemon
1 teaspoon turmeric
2 garlic cloves
2 dried chillies, crumbled
A handful of fresh mint
4 tablespoons natural yoghurt

Campfire Essentials:

Bamboo skewers pre-soaked for half an hour in water
  or sticks of fresh rosemary, as before

Put all the sauce ingredients except the yoghurt into a food processor and blitz until smooth. Stir in the yoghurt. You can then take the sauce to the campfire or barbecue in a ziplock bag.

Thread alternate pieces of fish and new potatoes onto the skewers or rosemary sprigs. Drizzle with the sauce and grill immediately for 2 minutes each side. Serve with any leftover sauce on the side.

VEGETABLES

Fried Wild Mushrooms with Crushed Garlic and Parsley, opposite

FRIED WILD MUSHROOMS WITH CRUSHED GARLIC AND PARSLEY

This works either as a side dish or as a topping for toast.

Serves 6
You will need:
A good knob of butter
2–3 fat garlic cloves, crushed to a paste
  with a pinch of sea salt
2–3 handfuls of wild mushrooms,
  such as field, chanterelles, ceps – whatever
  you've been lucky enough to find – broken up
  into similar-sized pieces (I was once told you
  should never cut a mushroom, but break or tear
  it into pieces with your fingers. Why, I've never
  found out, but I've always broken or torn my
  mushrooms this way ever since)
A handful of roughly chopped flat-leaf parsley
Sea salt and freshly ground black pepper

First, if you are having mushrooms on toast – get your toast ready, ideally on the grill over your fire (see p.146). Put the toast to one side, where it will stay warm – ready for its imminent topping. Drizzle with a little olive oil.

Melt the butter in a frying pan, add the garlic and, after a couple of minutes, the mushrooms. Keep them turning, well coated in garlicky butter, so that they don't char, and if necessary, move the frying pan so that it's not directly over the fire. Once they are done, stir in the parsley and season with sea salt and freshly ground black pepper. Pile the mushrooms onto the toast or serve as a side (they go well with chicken kebabs, steak or any barbecued meat).

Alternatively, stir 10 beaten eggs in the pan until they are just cooked, and you'll have turned a simple vegetable dish into a scrumptious mushroom scramble. This is also good on toasted sourdough. Serve with a simple green salad.

BAKED PORTOBELLO MUSHROOM CAPS WITH FETA AND TOMATO

This is great as a vegetarian main course too. The filling can be made at home and brought to the campsite in a plastic food container, to make things easier.

Serves 6
You will need:
12 portobello mushrooms
  (allow 2 per person for a main course)
For the filling:
Olive oil, for frying
3 fat garlic cloves, crushed to a paste
  with a pinch of sea salt
5 good handfuls of breadcrumbs
5 good handfuls of crumbled feta
6 medium tomatoes, diced into 1cm cubes
A good handful of roughly chopped
  flat-leaf parsley
Juice of 1-2 lemons
Sea salt and freshly ground black pepper
Unsalted butter
Campfire Essentials:
Aluminium foil

To make the filling, heat a couple of good slugs of olive oil in a frying pan, add the garlic, and cook for a couple of minutes. Add the breadcrumbs and fry them until they are golden. Tip the bread and garlic mixture into a bowl and add the feta, tomato, parsley and lemon juice, mixing well. Season with sea salt and freshly ground black pepper.

Stuff each mushroom cap with a couple of spoonfuls of the filling and dot with a knob of unsalted butter. Wrap in foil, and bake over the fire for about 20 minutes.

CRUSHED POTATOES

This is a good alternative to fried or mud-baked potatoes, and falls somewhere between a warm potato salad and bubble and squeak without the cabbage.

Serves 6
You will need:
4 waxy potatoes, peeled
   or scrubbed and cut into chunks
8–10 tablespoons olive oil
A handful of roughly chopped
   flat-leaf parsley or mint
Sea salt and freshly ground black pepper

Cook the potatoes in plenty of boiling salted water until they are tender, about 20 minutes. Drain them and set aside while you heat the oil.

Heat 4 good slugs of the olive oil in your frying pan. Tip the potatoes into the pan, and crush them with a fork while you fry them. Keep turning the crushed potatoes until they are brown on all sides, then remove the pan from the fire.

Pour the rest of the olive oil over the potatoes, stir in the parsley or mint, or both, and check the seasoning. This is equally good cold!

GRILLED CORN ON THE COB WITH SAGE AND BUTTER

Sage works very well when fried in butter – but you could equally well make the 'butter', and then use any kind of chopped fresh herb if you don't have sage to hand – just sprinkle onto the corn rather than crisping it first.

Serves 6
You will need:
6 corncobs
Olive oil, for rubbing
Sea salt and freshly ground black pepper
For the sage butter:
170g unsalted butter
A handful of sage leaves
5 slugs extra virgin olive oil
Juice of 1 lemon

Strip the corncobs of their outer husk and silk, give them a good rubbing of olive oil and season well with sea salt and freshly ground black pepper. Grill them for about 20 minutes, turning them so that they cook evenly all over. Remove them to a plate while you make the butter.

Put the butter into the frying pan, and melt it over the fire. Once the foaming has calmed down, add the sage leaves and fry until the leaves are crisp. Remove from the heat and add the olive oil. Add the lemon juice and spoon the mixture over the corn.

FRIED COURGETES WITH CHILLI AND LEMON

Every summer, we have almost more courgettes than we can eat: we grow them ourselves, we are given them by our neighbour who is also our plumber, and we are given them by The Hen Lady, nicknamed such because she happens to keep hens and I give her all the unwanted, uneaten ends of our baguettes for her hens. This is one of the many ways I cook the courgettes, and everyone loves their smoky, slightly spicy, lemony kick.

Serves 6
You will need:
Olive oil, for frying
3–4 fat garlic cloves, crushed
  with a pinch of sea salt
6–8 courgettes, sliced into thin rounds
A couple of pinches of crushed chillies
Zest and juice of 2 lemons
Sea salt and freshly ground black pepper

Warm a couple of slugs of olive oil in a big frying pan over a medium-hot bit of the fire, and add the garlic. Once it has started to brown a little, chuck in all the courgettes and let them cook away for about half an hour, stirring them every couple of minutes so they don't burn onto the bottom of the pan. Once they have really got going, you can move them off the hottest part of the fire. Add more olive oil if they are really sticking. They are done when they are a bit browned and well broken down, so that you have more of a mash.

Stir in the chillies and the lemon zest and juice, and check the seasoning. Serve hot or warm. They're good smeared onto bread and served as bruschetta, and with any barbecued meat.

PROPER BABA GANOUSH

This is the way baba ganoush is served in Jordan, Lebanon and Syria, as opposed to the auberginey tahini-infused mixture that we tend to call baba ganoush here. Aubergines grill brilliantly over a fire, so this is an ideal campfire recipe, even if it isn't a very obvious one! Excellent as either a side dish or a dip.

Serves 6
You will need:
4 medium aubergines
4 tomatoes, chopped into small chunks of about 1cm
Juice of 2 lemons
2 fat garlic cloves, crushed to a paste
  with a pinch of sea salt
2 teaspoons cumin
2 teaspoons sumac
A couple of slugs of olive oil
A good handful of roughly chopped flat-leaf parsley
Sea salt and freshly ground black pepper

Prick the aubergines all over to stop them exploding during cooking, and then grill them over the fire for about 45 minutes, turning them regularly, until the skin is black and blistered.

When they are cool enough to handle, peel the skin off them and discard it; now chop the flesh up in bowl - a knife and fork is easiest for this. If there is a lot of liquid, pour it off.

Stir in the chopped tomatoes, using your fingers if necessary, and add the lemon juice, garlic, cumin and sumac. Splash in the olive oil, check the seasoning and add the flat-leaf parsley. This is perfect with grilled meat, or as a dip with warm flatbreads (see p.225).

ONE-POT COOKING

Chorizo, Red Pepper, Tomato and Butter Bean Stew, p.213

CHICKEN SUMAC

Sumac is a red berry that grows in the mountains of Lebanon. Dried and ground, it is a tart, lemony spice that turns everything a wonderful shade of red. Za'atar is a fragrant mix of dried thyme, sumac, cumin, sesame seeds, salt and pepper. Both are used widely in Bedouin cooking.

Serves 6
You will need:
2 good handfuls of pine nuts
Olive oil, for frying
1 medium onion, finely chopped
2 fat garlic cloves, crushed to a paste
  with a pinch of sea salt
6 free-range chicken breasts, preferably organic
2 tablespoons sumac
1 tablespoon za'atar
A glass of water
Sea salt and freshly ground black pepper
A good handful of roughly chopped
  coriander leaves

Lightly toast your pine nuts in a hot, dry pan, until golden. Set aside.

Put a couple of good slugs of olive oil into your pot and heat gently over the fire, adding the onion and garlic after a minute or so. Once the onion is soft, remove from the heat and scoop out half the onion mixture into a bowl.

Add three of the chicken breasts to the pot, sprinkle with 1 tablespoon of the sumac, half a tablespoon of za'atar, a handful of pine nuts, a pinch of sea salt and freshly ground black pepper. Scatter over the remaining onion mixture and layer up the rest of the ingredients in the same way.

Add a glass of water and cover. Let it bubble away gently for about 20–30 minutes, until the chicken is cooked.

Sprinkle with fresh coriander and serve with crushed potatoes (see p.207) or mud-baked potatoes (see p.196) and a fresh green salad.

CHORIZO, RED PEPPER, TOMATO AND BUTTER BEAN STEW

I would normally never advocate using tinned beans, preferring the texture and flavour of any dried beans that have been soaked overnight and then cooked with fresh herbs and garlic and a splash of wine. However, I have used tinned butter beans here, for the sake of practicality and because the smokiness of the paprika infuses the beans with a delicious flavour.

Serves 6
You will need:
4 small cooking chorizos, mild or
  spicy depending on your taste
Olive oil, for frying
1 medium onion, finely chopped
2 fat garlic cloves, crushed to a paste
  with a pinch of sea salt
3–4 teaspoons smoked paprika
3 red peppers, deseeded and chopped
  into 2cm chunks
4 medium tomatoes, cut roughly into 8
A glass of water
2 x 400g tins butter beans, drained and rinsed
Sea salt and freshly ground black pepper
A good handful of chopped flat-leaf parsley

First of all, skin your chorizos and cut them into 5mm slices.

Put a couple of good slugs of olive oil into your pot and heat gently over the fire, adding the chorizo slices after a minute or so. Once browned on both sides, add the onion and garlic and cook gently until the onion has softened.

Stir in the smoked paprika and add the red peppers. After about 5 minutes, stir in the tomatoes and a glass of water, to loosen the mixture a little.

Cover and cook for another 10 minutes or so, then add the beans and give it all a good stir. Simmer another 5 minutes or so, for the beans to heat through.

Check the seasoning, stir in the parsley and serve with crushed potatoes (see p.207) or mud-baked potatoes (see p.196) and a green bean salad.

FISH AND SEAFOOD

Grilled Scallops with Asparagus and Prosciutto, opposite

GRILLED SCALLOPS WITH ASPARAGUS AND PROSCIUTTO

This is equally good without the prosciutto if you prefer a no-meat option.

Serves 6
You will need:
24 scallops
3–4 tablespoons olive oil
24–30 asparagus spears, woody ends cut off
18 slices prosciutto
2 good handfuls wild rocket
2 good handfuls baby spinach
Juice of 1–2 lemons
Sea salt and freshly ground black pepper
Campfire Essentials:
*Bamboo skewers pre-soaked for half an hour in water
or sticks of fresh rosemary, as p.200*

Wash the scallops and pat them dry with kitchen paper. You can do this at home and keep the scallops in an airtight container. I tend to cut off the coral, which I know some people think is a sacrilege, but none of us like them, so . . .

Heat some olive oil in a big frying pan and add the asparagus in batches. Cook each batch for a couple of minutes each side until slightly browned. Take them off the heat, and leave to cool.

Roll the slices of prosciutto into small cigar-shapes, and alternate 4 scallops and 3 prosciutto cigars on each skewer. Brush with olive oil and grill for about 10 minutes, turning frequently so that the scallops are crispy and brown on the outside but tender on the inside.

Put the rocket and spinach into a big bowl and dress with a couple of slugs of olive oil and the juice of 1 lemon. Season with a pinch of sea salt and freshly ground black pepper.

Serve the scallop skewers with the salad and asparagus, with another generous squeeze of lemon and drizzle of olive oil over the whole lot.

WHOLE FISH BAKED IN NEWSPAPER

I love this way of cooking fish – in an ideal world, the fish you would cook would be the brown trout you had caught yourself that afternoon . . . but any smallish, firm fish will do. Our favourites are trout and gilthead bream, but the choice is a very personal one. For the full method, see p.197.

You will need:
Small firm fish – whole and unfilleted
  (allow about 300g per person)
Sea salt and freshly ground black pepper
Optional seasoning of your choice
  (fresh herbs, lemon . . . it's up to you)
Campfire Essentials:
Plenty of newspaper
  (you'll need several sheets per fish)

Season each fish with sea salt and freshly ground black pepper, inside and out. You can also stuff the cavity with a bunch of fresh thyme, or rosemary, or even a wedge of lemon.

Wrap each fish in about 5 half sheets of newspaper, wetting each sheet first. It is important to do it this way, which is slightly more labour intensive, but is more effective and easier to handle than a wedge of wet newspaper.

Cook the fish on the grill for about 15 minutes a side, occasionally sprinkling the parcels with water. The parcels will blacken but will not catch fire, but if you feel unsure, keep a bottle of water nearby. Take the parcels off the grill and cut them open. The skin should come away with the paper and you will be left with deliciously melting fish.

Serve with fried courgettes (see p.209), and a grilled flatbread per person (see p.225) to mop up any juices.

WHOLE FISH STEAMED IN WILD GRASS

Like the whole fish baked in newspaper, this is a deceptively simple way of cooking fish. I first got the idea of cooking fish this way from Annie Bell's lovely *The Camping Cookbook* (Kyle Cathie).

You will need:
Medium-sized fish – whole and unfilleted
  (allow about 300g per person)
Sea salt and freshly ground black pepper
Optional seasoning of your choice
  (garlic, lemon zest, fresh herbs . . .)
Campfire Essentials:
Plenty of wild grass

Season each fish with sea salt and freshly ground black pepper. You can fill the cavity with a bunch of fresh thyme or rosemary, and you can also score the fish diagonally and stuff the slits with some slices of garlic, slices of lemon zest or some more herbs.

Cook the fish on grass as on p.196.

The cooking time depends on the size of the fish, but allow between 20 and 30 minutes a side. Serve with a squeeze of lemon and a fresh green salad.

MEAT AND POULTRY

Lamb Chops with Honey and Mustard, opposite

LAMB CHOPS WITH HONEY AND MUSTARD

The honey and mustard glaze makes these chops deliciously sweet and sticky – and very popular with children (and adults) as you can eat them with your hands. You could also try the glaze, with or without the rosemary, on chicken drumsticks.

Serves 6
A couple of sprigs of fresh rosemary,
  leaves picked and chopped
About 6 tablespoons honey
  and mustard glaze (see p.232)
12 lamb chops (2 per person)
3-4 fat garlic cloves, thinly sliced
Olive oil
Sea salt and freshly ground black pepper

First, mix the chopped rosemary into the glaze. Then make a couple of incisions into each side of each chop and stick in a slice of garlic. Rub the chops with olive oil and season with sea salt and freshly ground black pepper.

Grill the chops for about 5 minutes each side, and then brush generously on both sides with the glaze and grill for another 3-4 minutes each side. The chops will be smokily sticky on the outside and just a bit pink on the inside.

CHICKEN IN YOGHURT MARINADE

This is great on chicken but works well on fish, too.

Serves 6
You will need:
6 free-range chicken breasts, preferably organic
For the marinade:
4 tablespoons natural yoghurt
2 fat garlic cloves, crushed to a paste
*   with a pinch of sea salt*
A good handful of fresh mint leaves
A good handful of fresh coriander leaves
A small knob of fresh ginger,
*   peeled and roughly chopped*
Juice of 1 lemon
2 teaspoons ground cumin
A pinch of cayenne or crushed dried chillies
Sea salt and freshly ground black pepper

The easiest way to make this marinade is to put all the ingredients into a food processor and whizz until smooth. Tip the marinade into a large ziplock bag, add the chicken breasts, whole, and zip the bag shut securely and turn it over until all the chicken is coated. Leave for at least an hour, but more is better and overnight is best. Keep chilled.

When you're ready to cook, take the chicken breasts out of the marinade and grill for 10-15 minutes each side. A cucumber and yoghurt salad is really lovely with this, as a cooler.

GRILLED MARINATED STEAK WITH YOGHURT MINT SAUCE

Of course you can just grill these steaks without bothering with the marinating bit, but the marinade does tenderise the beef and makes it taste, well, just that little bit nicer. You can also use individual steaks instead of a whole piece. All you need do is adjust the cooking time accordingly.

Serves 6
You will need:
1.5kg flank steak
4-6 tablespoons essential marinade (see p.232)
For the yoghurt mint sauce:
4 good tablespoons natural yoghurt
2 good handfuls of chopped fresh mint
1 tablespoon olive oil
Sea salt and freshly ground black pepper

Put the marinade ingredients into a large ziplock bag, add the flank steak and give it a good shake, making sure that the zip is properly shut, until the steak is coated with the marinade. Leave for at least an hour, somewhere cool, but more is better and overnight is best.

When you're ready to cook, take the steak out of the marinade and grill for 6-10 minutes on each side, depending on how well you like it cooked. When it's done to your liking, put it onto a board, cover it with foil and leave it to rest for 5-10 minutes, while you stir together the ingredients for the yoghurt sauce.

Slice the steak into thin slices, and serve with a dollop of the minty yoghurt.

GRILLED STEAK WITH 5-SPICE RUB

I use Chinese 5 spice (usually a blend of cinnamon, star anise, fennel, cloves and ginger) as a rub for steaks if I'm looking for something a bit different. It is readily available anywhere that sells herbs and spices.

Serves 6
You will need:
6 rump steaks
For the rub:
1 tablespoon Chinese 5 spice
1 tablespoon brown sugar
1 tablespoon grated fresh ginger
About 1 tablespoon olive oil

Mix the dry ingredients together, then add the ginger and enough olive oil to give the mixture a paste-like consistency. Then rub the steaks with the mixture, making sure they are well covered. Hands are the best implements for this.

Grill the steaks for 5 minutes or so each side, depending on how you like them cooked.

Serve with crushed potatoes (see p.207) and a fresh green salad.

VENISON STEAK WITH JUNIPER AND THYME

The first time we ever made this we had a huge amount of people at Glen Dye for lunch. It was on the weekend of our daughter India's christening and a friend had given us a loin of venison as a gift ...

Serves 6
You will need:
6 venison steaks, or 1.5kg venison loin
Olive oil, for drizzling
Sea salt and freshly ground black pepper
For the marinade:
10 juniper berries, crushed
3 fat garlic cloves, crushed to a paste with a pinch of sea salt
A good handful of fresh thyme leaves
600ml red wine
Campfire essentials:
Aluminium foil, for the venison loin

A note about venison: roe deer - because it lives on low ground, and doesn't have to clamber up hillsides - is the more tender meat. Red deer lives on higher ground and eats heather - it can taste heathery, is gamier than roe and is generally tougher, so it needs to marinate a little longer.

Mix all the marinade ingredients together and tip into a ziplock bag. Add the venison and, making sure that the zip is properly shut, turn the bag upside down to coat the meat in the marinade. Leave to marinate somewhere cool for at least 3 hours, but overnight is best,

Remove the venison from the marinade, drizzle with olive oil and grill the steaks for about 5 minutes each side, depending on how well you like it done.

If you're cooking the whole loin, drizzle with olive oil, season with a little sea salt, and wrap it in foil. Cook it over the fire for 20-30 minutes, and then let it rest for about 5 minutes before unwrapping and carving.

Serve with crushed potatoes (see p.207).

BILL GRANGER'S CHICKEN BURGERS WITH LEMONGRASS AND LIME

This recipe comes from our friend and neighbour, the Australian chef and food writer Bill Granger.

Serves 6
You will need:
600g minced chicken
1 onion, finely grated
85g fresh white breadcrumbs
1 garlic clove, crushed
1 lemongrass stalk (white part only),
finely chopped
2 tablespoons chopped fresh coriander
2 tablespoons finely grated lime zest
1 tablespoon fish sauce
2 teaspoons caster sugar
For serving:
Soft rolls
Lettuce leaves
Fresh mint and coriander leaves
Chilli sauce
Spicy slaw (see p.231)

Put the chicken mince, onion, breadcrumbs, garlic, lemongrass, coriander, lime zest, fish sauce and sugar in a large bowl and mix together well with your hands. Shape into 6 patties, then cover and refrigerate for 30 minutes.

Preheat a barbecue or chargrill pan and brush with a little light-flavoured oil such as grapeseed. Cook the patties for 4 minutes each side or until cooked through. Serve on soft rolls with lettuce, mint and coriander leaves and chilli sauce. Great with spicy slaw.

FLATBREADS

Flatbread Sandwiches, p.227

BASIC FLATBREADS

Jack, our eldest son, has been into cooking since he was about 15. He is the king of campfire flatbreads and makes them pretty much whenever we have a campfire. This is his recipe.

Makes 8 flatbreads
You will need:
500g strong white bread flour, preferably organic
1 teaspoon quick yeast
1 teaspoon fine salt
1 teaspoon caster sugar
1 tablespoon organic sunflower oil,
  plus small slug of oil
300ml warm water

Put all the dry ingredients into a big bowl, make a well in the middle, and pour in the sunflower oil and the warm water. Starting from the middle, gradually incorporate all the dry ingredients until it forms a dough. Tip the dough out onto a floured surface and knead for about 15 minutes, until the dough is smooth and elastic. Put a small slug of oil into a clean bowl, add the dough and cover with a damp tea towel or cling film. Leave to rise in a warm place for about an hour, until more or less doubled in size.

Punch down the dough, tip it out onto a floured surface and knead for another 5 minutes or so. Divide the ball roughly into 8, and roll each bit into a ball shape before flattening it out with either a floured rolling pin, or squashing and pulling it gently with your hands.

At this stage, you can flavour the flatbreads – poke in a few rosemary tips or garlic slivers and brush with olive oil, sprinkle with nigella seeds, or even a za'atar and olive oil paste.

Flour each flatbread well to stop them sticking together, and take them to the campfire between two damp tea towels or in a plastic container.

Grill for 3–4 minutes each side, making sure they don't burn. Serve immediately.

FLATBREAD SANDWICHES

Once your flatbreads are cooked, you can make them into wonderful sandwiches. Try grilled steak with a dollop of mustard and a handful of rocket, or a couple of grilled sausages, a grilled tomato half and a cos lettuce leaf, or a grilled sliced chicken breast with homemade basil mayonnaise and a grilled red pepper half. A great vegetarian option is a grilled red pepper half, a grilled tomato half, a dollop of home-made pesto and a handful of rocket.

FLATBREAD PIZZAS

As improbable as it sounds, pizzas made this way work really well. Smear the uncooked flatbread with tomato purée, or sliced fresh tomatoes, and scatter over some torn mozzarella and then add whatever other toppings you like.

Put the pizza on the grill for about 5 minutes, until the mozzarella has melted. Don't put the pizzas directly over the flames or the bases will burn - keep them on one side or on a cooler part of the fire.

SOMETHING SWEET

S'mores, opposite

BAKED CHOCOLATE BANANAS

Keeping the skin on, slit 1 banana per person lengthways through the skin and into the fruit, and pop in 3 or 4 squares of chocolate: white, milk or dark (Green & Black's is our family preference). Wrap each banana in foil and bake over the fire for about 5 minutes on each side.

Unwrap and unpeel the bananas – carefully – and serve with a dollop of double cream or crème fraiche for that little extra . . .

SWEET AND STICKY FIGS

Allowing a couple of figs per person, cut the figs in half and dip each half in water or lemon juice, and then in caster sugar. Grill the figs for a couple of minutes each side and serve with a dollop of crème fraiche.

S'MORES

There are a hundred different ways of making this all-time American classic. This is our way. Why s'mores? You'll see . . .

For each s'more you will need:
2 marshmallows
2 digestive biscuits
An 8-square block of Green & Black's
  milk chocolate

Toast the marshmallows over the fire until they are slightly charred and gooey inside. Put one marshmallow onto a digestive, squash it down with the block of chocolate, put the other marshmallow on top and carefully squash on the second digestive. The hot marshmallow will melt the chocolate . . . what s'more can I say?

ESSENTIALS

Spicy Slaw, opposite

BILL GRANGER'S SPICY SLAW

This is another recipe from our friend Bill Granger. It goes fantastically well with his chicken burgers or with any grilled fish, lamb or chicken dishes.

Serves 10
You will need:
2 tablespoons caster sugar
2 tablespoons rice vinegar or white vinegar
2 large carrots, peeled and cut into
    thin matchsticks
2 large handfuls of shredded white cabbage
2 large handfuls of shredded red cabbage
4 celery sticks, trimmed and cut into
    thin matchsticks
1 large red onion, thinly sliced
A large handful of fresh Vietnamese
    mint leaves (or ordinary mint leaves)
A large handful of fresh coriander leaves
For the sweet chilli dressing:
1 tablespoon rice vinegar or white vinegar
1 tablespoon caster sugar
1½ tablespoons lime juice
2 tablespoons fish sauce
2 long red chillies, seeded and finely chopped
½ teaspoon sea salt

Mix together the sugar and rice vinegar, add the carrot and leave to marinate for 20 minutes.

Put the white and red cabbage in a large mixing bowl. Drain the carrot and add to the cabbage with the celery, onion, mint and coriander.

Mix together all the dressing ingredients, stirring until the sugar has dissolved. Add the dressing to the salad and toss together. Store in an airtight container in the fridge or a cool box.

ESSENTIAL MARINADE

This marinade is excellent for meat and fish as it is, but you can also add any dried herb to dress it up a bit.

Makes enough for 8
You will need:
Juice of 2-3 lemons
4-5 tablespoons olive oil
2-3 fat garlic cloves, crushed to a paste
  with a pinch of sea salt
Sea salt and some freshly ground black pepper

Mix all the ingredients together and store in an airtight plastic container in the fridge or a cool box. This also works as a salad dressing, on its own, or combined with some honey and mustard glaze (see below).

HONEY AND MUSTARD GLAZE

Mix 4 tablespoons of Dijon mustard, either grainy or smooth, with 4 tablespoons of set honey. Store in an airtight container. This makes enough glaze for 8 chicken breasts or 16 lamb chops.

WHITE WINE, ROSEMARY AND GARLIC MARINADE

This marinade works best for chicken and fish, but it also works well for red meats.

Makes enough for 6 to 8
You will need:
A glass of white wine
A sprig of rosemary, leaves stripped and chopped
2 fat garlic cloves, crushed to a paste
  with a pinch of salt
4-6 good slugs olive oil
Sea salt and some freshly ground black pepper

Mix all the ingredients together and store in an airtight plastic container.

PICNIC FOOD

Parma Ham, Mozzarella and Avocado Rolls, p.235

PICNIC FOOD

~ CAROLINE ~

As is so often the case with the great outdoors, picnic food is a question of trial and error. It has taken a fair amount of errors over the years, especially when the children were younger, but I now have some pretty fail-safe favourites that work every time.

The key to success seems to be to have things that require the least amount of equipment in terms of plates and cutlery and so on; in other words, things that can be eaten on the hoof. An early mistake was trying to get the children to sit down on the picnic rug and eat off plates. It usually ended up with food on the rug, or the plates simply abandoned, much to the delight of the ever-hungry dogs, while the children rushed off to do something more interesting.

The advantage of having 'finger food' is that there is a lot less stuff that you have to remember to bring – no plates, no cutlery, and very little messy washing-up, which is always the worst bit about coming home from a picnic.

Here are a few of our top picnic ideas.

STICKY SAUSAGES

Although you can of course just have cold plain sausages, these are simple to make and worth the extra effort, transforming something fairly ordinary into something lip-smackingly delicious!

Makes enough for 8
You will need:
Your favourite sausages
(Cumberland, wild boar, venison,
Italian veal and herb . . .)
A portion of honey and mustard glaze (see p.232)

Coat the sausages with the glaze and then cook them as normal. Cool, wrap and enjoy!

PARMA HAM, MOZZARELLA AND AVOCADO ROLLS

These scrumptious snacks are easy to assemble, easy to transport and easy to eat! Allow at least 4 per person.

Makes enough for 8
You will need:
A thick slice of buffalo mozzarella
A slice of avocado
A slice of Parma ham

Stack the mozzarella and avocado slices on top of each other at one end of the slice of Parma ham and roll it up. Yes it is that simple! (It's best to assemble these once you're at your picnic destination, or the avocado will brown.)

CALZONES (FOLDED-OVER PIZZAS)

The great thing about calzones is that, like pizzas, you can fill them with whatever you like, so you can either make a whole batch of simple Margheritas, or you can do something more elaborate. But, unlike standard pizzas, they're brilliantly portable – a bit like Cornish pasties. I have sometimes taken individual orders and then initialled each calzone at the cooking stage, with a beaten egg and a pastry brush – or with a bit of extra dough, made into the initial and stuck on with a bit of beaten egg.

Makes 8 calzones
You will need:
1kg strong white bread flour, preferably organic
2 teaspoons quick yeast
2 teaspoons fine salt
2 teaspoons caster sugar
2 tablespoons sunflower oil
600ml warm water
The filling of your choice (see below)

Put all the dry ingredients into a bowl, add all the oil and warm water and mix to a dough with your hands. Once all the ingredients have come together, tip the contents out onto a floured work surface and knead them together for about 20 minutes until the dough is smooth and elastic. You can also do this in the bowl of your mixer, with the dough hook attachment. Once you are happy with the consistency of your dough, put an extra slug of oil into the bottom of your bowl, pop the dough ball back in and cover it with cling film. Leave it in a warm place to rise for a couple of hours.

While the dough is rising, you can get your fillings ready. Here are some suggestions, but it is really a question of personal taste:

Tomato purée
(as a base, not on its own)
Mozzarella, sliced or grated
Parma ham
Ham
Rocket
Cooked spinach
Parmesan
Tuna
Mushrooms
Roast red peppers, cut into strips

Once the dough has doubled in size, take off the cling film, punch down the dough (very therapeutic!) and turn it out onto a floured surface. Knead it again for about 5 minutes and then divide it into 8 balls. Meanwhile, preheat the oven to 180°C/gas mark 4.

Taking one ball at a time (cover the rest with a damp, clean tea towel), roll it out on a well-floured work surface, until you have a circle about 3mm thick. Spread tomato purée over the whole circle, leaving about 1cm round the edge.

Add your toppings of choice to one half, but be careful not to overfill. Dampen the edges, either with a pastry brush dipped in milk, or just use your fingers. Then fold over the dough to make a half-moon shape and squash the edges together with the prongs of a fork. Make a little hole in the dough so that the air can escape while the calzone is cooking, and if you are initialling the calzone, now is the time to do it.

Pop the finished calzone onto a floured baking tray and bake it for about 10-15 minutes on each side. While it is cooking, get on with making the next one. If you are doing a whole batch with the same fillings, you can do 4 at a time, and cook them all together. Once they are golden brown and smelling delicious, leave them to cool on a cooling rack.

When they are cool, you can either wrap them in foil, or put them in an airtight plastic container, picnic-ready.

COURGETTE AND FETA TART

I came up with this winning combination in France one year when we had a particular glut of courgettes and I was thinking of ways of using them up. You can use ready-made pastry, but home-made shortcrust pastry is simple to make, takes no time, and tastes much better. I never blind-bake (pre-bake) the pastry when I make this, but you can if you prefer.

You will need:
For the pastry:
450g plain flour
A pinch of salt
225g unsalted butter, straight from
  the fridge and cut into cubes
A glass of cold water
For the filling:
4–6 courgettes, washed, topped and tailed
2 x 200g blocks feta cheese, preferably organic
4 tablespoons natural yoghurt
8 eggs, beaten
A good pinch of nutmeg
Sea salt and freshly ground black pepper
Equipment:
A roasting tin measuring about 25.5 x 30cm

Put the flour and salt into your food processor and turn it on. Add the butter, a cube at a time. When the mixture resembles breadcrumbs, add the water gradually, until the dough starts to clump together. Alternatively, to do this by hand, rub the butter into the flour and salt with your fingertips to form breadcrumbs, then add the water slowly, stirring it in with a knife.

Turn the dough out onto a well-floured surface and roll.

Grease the roasting tin and line with the pastry, trim off the edges and prick the bottom with a fork. Put it to rest in the fridge while you make the filling, and preheat your oven to 180°C/gas mark 4.

Grate the courgettes into a big bowl, roughly chop or crumble the feta and add to the bowl.

In a separate bowl, beat the yoghurt into the eggs, add the nutmeg and season with salt and pepper (bearing in mind that feta is already quite salty). Add this to the courgettes and feta, stir, then tip into the chilled pastry case, spreading it out evenly.

Bake for about 30-40 minutes, until it is set and golden. Leave to cool completely before cutting.

Serve with a big bowl of fresh and garlicky green salad as a delicious and easy summer lunch or supper.

ORANGE AND WHITE CHOCOLATE CAKE

Surely no picnic is complete without something sweet, and this cake does it all. The Rose Bakery's *Breakfast, Lunch and Tea* (Phaidon) is one of my most well-thumbed cookery books; one day I added white chocolate to their orange cake recipe and this was the result. It also goes beautifully with raspberries and a good dollop of crème fraiche adds the finishing touch.

You will need:
2 unwaxed oranges, left whole
1 unwaxed lemon, left whole
200g Green & Black's white chocolate
6 eggs
450g golden caster sugar
550g ground almonds
1 teaspoon baking powder
Equipment:
You can either cook this in a 23cm
 springform cake tin, or in 2 x 1lb loaf tins. I
 prefer to use the loaf tins, with paper loaf tin
 liners (you can get them from Lakeland, or any
 good kitchen shop), as it is easier to have loaf
 slices for a picnic.

Grease the cake tin and line the base with baking parchment (or pop your paper liners in your loaf tins).

Put the oranges and lemon in a saucepan with enough water to cover them. Put a lid on the pan, place over a medium high heat and, once the water is boiling, reduce the heat and simmer for about an hour until the fruit is soft.

Once soft, remove the fruit from the heat and drain. When the fruit is cool enough to handle, slice in half and take out the pips. Then blitz the fruit, skin and all, to a smooth purée in your food processor.

Preheat your oven to 180°C/gas mark 4.

Break the white chocolate into pieces and melt in a bowl suspended over a pan of simmering water. Set aside to cool slightly.

In another bowl, beat the eggs and sugar together until they are just combined. Add the fruit purée and then stir in the melted chocolate. Once the mixture is smooth, add the ground almonds and the baking powder. Combine well and then tip the mixture into the cake tin or loaf tins.

Bake for about 35-45 minutes, until golden brown and a skewer inserted into the middle of the cake comes out clean. I sometimes have to cover the cake with foil halfway through the cooking to stop the top from burning. Let the cake cool completely before turning it out of the tin.

WHAT TO BUY AND WHERE

Notes

THE BEST KIT FOR THE GREAT OUTDOORS

Buy cheap, buy twice. We are both interested in design and we have lived in the Highlands for more than 20 years, so we have really learnt about the best kit for the great outdoors. Here are some of our favourite, tried and tested things.

~ AXES & SAWS ~

~ Axes ~
Casstrom.co.uk; Gransfors.com; Bestmadeco.com; Basecampx.com

The best European axes are made by either Casström or Gränsfors Bruks. Both of these companies have been making axes for ages.

In the US, the newcomer Best Made Company makes the most exquisite axes, often in limited runs and with wonderful painted handles. Base Camp X is based in Canada and makes our favourite throwing axes. (For more on axes, see p.147.)

~ Hatchets ~
Estwingtools.co.uk

Caroline's Estwing camping hatchet is the best thing for splitting kindling that we have ever owned. It's forged from a single piece of hardened steel and has a leather grip to absorb shock. Made in Rockford, Illinois by Estwing, who makes other excellent tools, too.

~ Saws ~
Opinel.com; Trailblazerproducts.com

Opinel makes the best French pocket knives; these are a must-buy for every schoolboy who visits a French market, but they are good for grown ups, too. We have a folding Opinel saw. There are two sizes available and the larger of the two, with an 18cm blade, is the most efficient. If you're looking for something larger then it's hard to beat Trailblazer's Take-Down Bucksaw, which is manufactured in Ontario using steel and aluminium. Bucksaws are ideal for felling trees and cutting firewood, but most are not collapsible. This is and this – combined with its high quality components – makes it an ideal camping companion.

~ BAGS & BLANKETS ~

~ Bags and backpacks ~
Chapmanbags.com; Billingham.co.uk

Our favourite everyday, all-weather shoulder bags are made by Billingham They are unbelievably robust and almost completely waterproof. Because we love them so much, Billingham agreed to make bags for us at Pedlars; and they sell like hot cakes.

Billingham makes the finest camera bags in the world, although when Martin Billingham founded the company in 1973, it only made fishing bags. But within a few years Billingham discovered that photographers, mainly from New York, had appropriated the bags. Mr Billingham himself was a keen photographer and so, in 1978, he switched all his production to camera bags. The rest is history; pretty much every famous photographer of the last 40 years has used a Billingham. The company is now run by Harry Billingham, the founder's son. The bags are perfect for outdoor people, even if you don't take pictures.

If you're looking for a specific fishing or game bag, then you can't beat John Chapman's bags. Chapman specialises in high-quality bags, all of which are made in Carlisle in Cumbria.

~ Rucksacks ~

Duluthpack.com; Filson.com; Fjallraven.se

For comfort and efficiency out and about in the wild, a rucksack (or backpack) is the thing.

Some of our favourites are: vintage Lafuma – French, canvas and leather, sometimes with a support frame. The original and the best. Vintage Swiss army rucksacks are good, too, particularly those from the 1960s. (Why is it that the Swiss army has so much cool stuff?) Both rucksacks often pop up on eBay or in flea markets and often cost only a few pounds. Duluth Pack makes a huge range of waterproof canvas backpacks in the US, all of which are great. Duluth does ship to the UK but, with taxes, it will not be cheap. Try Wardstones.co.uk, or find yourself a friendly American. Fjällräven is a Swedish company that makes wonderful lightweight rucksacks (and other outdoor gear). We use ours a lot – and love it – although I am not sure that it is as waterproof as it should be. And, finally, we like Filson canvas backpacks, too. These are made in Seattle and have been since the late 1800s. Sometimes we wish that an empty Filson bag wasn't quite so heavy – the canvas is very thick – but they do the job well.

~ Blankets – for picnics, horses and dogs ~

*Witneybedding.co.uk; Fridayfox.co.uk:
Hbc.com; Pendleton-usa.com*

Most houses in rural areas have a picnic blanket or two. We have several but our favourite is made in England by Early's of Witney and has a really strong, waterproof backing. Witney, in Oxfordshire, has been famous for its blankets since the Middle Ages and makes arguably the most famous horse blankets in the world. The company also makes dog coats and all of these are made from the same, distinctive, striped wool. A number of good, thick, classic wool blankets are made in the US. Special mention should go to the Hudson Bay Company for its striped Hbc point blanket and to Pendleton, especially for its Yakima Camp Blanket.

~ CLOTHING ~

~ Coats ~

*Barbourbymail.co.uk; Harristweed.org;
Breanishtweed.co.uk*

Barbour is good, of course; we like the simple, original waxed version best although it takes a decade of use to look good and is impractical for cold weather or on a hot day.

Recent developments have meant that tweed has been somewhat overlooked as outdoor protection in favour of hi-tech fabrics. But tweed is incredibly windproof and waterproof as well as rip-proof and will last for decades. Good enough for Mallory and our dads; good enough for anyone. (See p.158 for more on Mallory's clothing.) The key is to get good tweed and some of the best is Harris Tweed, protected under trademark by the Harris Tweed Authority and woven only at three mills in the Outer Hebrides. The revitalised Breanish Tweed, also in the Outer Hebrides, is – at the time of writing – offering customers the chance to commission their own tweed in runs of only 12m.

~ Weatherproof jackets ~
Canada-goose.com; Filson.com; Schoffel.co.uk;
Aspesi.com; Veilance.arcteryx.com

Canada Goose makes the best heavy winter jackets we have ever owned. We also swear by Schöffel's breathable, waterproof stuff and most of our Scottish friends seem to agree. Filson in Seattle (see also rucksacks) makes some brilliant coats too; my Filson hunting jacket seems to be completely unbreakable. Arc'teryx Veilance makes extraordinary lightweight, breathable, warm and weatherproof jackets in Vancouver. I have one of its Insulator Jackets and find that it offers the best base layer for freezing weather. Arc'teryx Veilance also makes backpacks and although I have never used one, I imagine that they are great. I should also mention Aspesi, which uses Thermore - a polyester padding that really does keep your body at its natural temperature - to make the amazing overshirts beloved of chic Italian scooter riders. Caroline has a brilliant cycling cape made by Aspesi which is as good for walking the dogs on a wild and windy day as it is for keeping dry on a bicycle.

~ Hats ~
Lockhatters.co.uk; Pedlars.co.uk

When I was young I thought that the idea of wearing a hat to keep warm was absurd. My parents would tell me that half of my body heat, or something, was lost through my head (this turns out to be a complete myth, in fact, as you only lose more heat through your head than through the rest of the body if you are not wearing anything on your head and are otherwise fully clothed). Anyway, now I am a proper, grown-up countryman, I very rarely go outside in the country without a hat.

My favourite hats are tweed caps made by Lock & Co., who has been making hats since 1676. Some of its hats are now manufactured in Portugal, but many are still made in England - of proper Scottish tweed - and although they are expensive, they are beautifully made. They keep me warm and are waterproof too. Locks also makes some cashmere beanies for us at Pedlars, although this is not part of the standard range.

~ Riding hats ~
Hut-kaufen.de

The Mayser Wind Rose riding hat is a German, cowboy-style hat that is perfect if you are riding long distances in heat or rain; it not only provides protection from the sun, but looks good, is completely waterproof and can include a built in helmet and chinstrap. Caroline has a brown version, and it is also available in black and green.

~ Jumpers ~
Guernseyknitwear.co.uk; Aransweatermarket.com

Guernseys are our favourite jumpers. Made in Guernsey, they have remained pretty much unchanged since the 17th century. They are water-resistant due to their highly twisted wool and elaborate stitching, and are also warm and very robust. Caroline has one that she bought with saved-up pocket money when she was 15, and she still wears it for riding today. Aran sweaters are wonderful, too, and robust. Made in the Aran Isles, off western Ireland, these were traditionally worn by fishermen, who benefited from their unscoured wool that retained its lanolin and so was waterproof.

~ Socks ~
Almostunwearoutable.com; Eskvalleyknitwear.com

Our favourite outdoor socks are made in Britain. Almost Unwearoutable has been making socks in Northumberland for over 30 years; these are the best thick wellie socks imaginable and - as the name suggests - they are remarkably robust. Esk Valley Knitwear, established in 1969, right in the south of Scotland, also makes some brilliant socks.

~ Gloves ~
Ircglove.com

There are masses of hi-tech gloves available; in fact you've probably got some that are warm and waterproof. But nothing beats a deerskin glove. Deerskin is extremely strong and yet very flexible. The very best deerskin gloves are made in the US, by J R Churchill, who has been making gloves since the late 1800s. I have only used its basic Thinsulate-lined gloves; but if motorcycling, falconry or rodeo are your thing, then Churchill has the gloves for you.

~ Waterproof overtrousers ~
Schoffel.co.uk

We have drawers full of these at home, mainly in now-grown-out-of children's sizes. They are essential if children are going to survive cheerfully in rain or snow. Specialist ski gear aside, the best pairs we have are made by Schöffel because they are fully breathable (so you don't roast in them) as well as wind- and waterproof.

~ Walking boots ~
Diemmefootwear.com

We love walking but are no experts on walking boots, generally favouring wellies for short walks and trainers for longer ones. However, the best walking boots we have found are by Diemme. These are excellent, beautifully-made and ridiculously comfortable boots for kicking around in during winter (Charlie wore a pair for several months last year). And they look good, too. Diemme boots are made in Montebelluna in Italy, which is the world capital of quality hiking and ski boot manufacture.

~ Wellies ~
Muckbootcompany.com

A good pair of wellies is probably the most important thing you will ever own in the countryside.

We all swear by Muckboots. They are cheap, exceptionally warm (you will never get cold feet in these) and long-lasting. They were originally developed in the late 1990s for use in some of the colder reaches of the US. They are made of a rubber foam - a bit like neoprene to you and I - and this is fantastic for keeping feet warm. You can fold them down in summer, which means that you won't ever get too sweaty in Muckboots. There are also some excellent wellies made in Scandinavia. Simple, unlined rubber boots are fine for summer but a disaster in winter as they will not keep your feet warm. Expensive, leather-lined boots - and indeed some European models with thin neoprene lining - are pretty useless in the countryside.

~ Work boots ~
Blundstone.com; Redwingshoes.com

Beyond wellies and walking boots, a good pair of work boots is useful for kicking around in outside. The best, we think, are either the iconic Australian Blundstones or Red Wing. Blundstones (or Blunnies) are now made in Tasmania, but the company originated in England. Its elasticated ankle boots and rigger boots are faultless, strong and easy to slip on and off. Red Wing boots have been made in Red Wing Minnesota since 1903; they come in a phenomenal array of shapes, but are mainly leather and they really do last for a very long time. Red Wing offers an excellent repair service (in the US) for old boots.

~ Boot care ~
Ejeffries.co.uk; Otterwax.com

We use Jeffries Leathercare, which is made in England, for the horses' tack but it is good for outdoor boots too. Otter Wax, made in Portland, Oregon, is an all-natural, non-toxic, fabric-protecting wax for canvas and many other types of cotton. Otter Wax also offers an entirely natural salve for leather.

~ COOKING & EATING ~

~ Enamelware ~
Labourandwait.co.uk; Falconenamelware.com

Nothing beats enamelware for outdoor use. Enamelware is glass fused onto heavy-gauge steel. It is smooth, tough and holds colour exceptionally well.

Much of this used to be made in Britain, but very little, if any, is now. The best-quality enamelware is made by Reiss in Austria; this is available in a vast range of colours. It is expensive, but heavy and of the finest quality. Falcon Enamelware produces a good range of classic vibrant white bowls and beakers.

~ Flasks and horn cups ~
Wentworth-pewter.com

Horn cups are lovely things that seem well suited to outdoor living, being lightweight and almost unbreakable. A few manufacturers, especially of buffalo horn, in India still make them, although we've found all of ours at flea markets. Match them with whisky from a Wentworth pewter flask, made in Sheffield since 1949.

~ Salt and pepper container ~
Swiss-advance.com

As you know, our mantra for campfire cooking is 'keep it simple'. However, salt and pepper are essential in good cooking and so you'll probably want to take these ingredients with you to your tent. The Swiss Spice Advance Classic Shaker is a compact, lightweight, strong, simple, humidity-proof utensil that we never go camping without. It is a relatively new design, but already something of a classic.

~ Titanium spork ~
Pedlars.co.uk

In recent years the spork – part fork, part spoon, part serrated knife – has become a crucial part of any camper's kit. Most are plastic, but the titanium one is the best; lightweight, incredibly strong and strangely elegant.

~ Kendal Mint Cake ~
Pedlars.co.uk

The original, iconic high-energy snack for outdoor people. Kendal was the first mint cake to be carried to the summit of Everest in 1953 and was eaten there by Sir Edmund Hilary and Sirdar Tensing. Still manufactured in Kendal, by George Romney Ltd, it is made by combining sugar (white or brown), glucose and water with a touch of peppermint oil. Good for adults and an excellent lure for grumbling children, too.

~ BALMS ~

Hudsalva balm
Apoteket.se; Missingsweden.com

Like many great cosmetics, this has a wide range of uses. We first discovered it when it was recommended as a foot balm; indeed, it was originally developed to soothe blisters on the feet of the Swedish army (it is called Försvarets Hudsalva, which means something like 'the military skin cream'). More recently it has become the go-to balm for sore Swedish lips. Almost every Swede we have encountered uses this during the winter to soothe their lips. It tastes and smells of a gentle vanilla. It is also, apparently, good for frying food, if no other oil is available, and is – allegedly – sometimes used by the Swedish army as a multi-purpose mechanical oil.

Available at the Swedish pharmacy chain, Apoteket.se, although you may need to call them (or go to Sweden) as the website is difficult to navigate unless you live in Sweden/ speak Swedish. You could also try the more English language-friendly: Missingsweden. com

~ KNIVES ~

~ Mushroom knives ~
Opinel.com

If you're going foraging for mushrooms you really should use a proper mushroom knife, so that you can cut the mushroom on its stalk rather than yanking the whole thing out of the ground and, therefore, giving it a chance to propagate. Opinel makes excellent folding knives with natural brushes and a measuring scale on the handle.

~ Penknives ~
Victorinox.com; Laguiole.com

These have to be Swiss army, for complex bits and pieces (and that essential thing for getting stones out of horses hooves) or – for simplicity and elegant efficiency – an Opinel (for more on Opinel, see entries on mushroom knives and saws). Alternatively, look out for genuine Laguiole knives, made in the knife-making capital of Europe. There are loads of fake Laguiole knives around, made in China, so try not to be fooled. The real McCoy will last forever and is ruthlessly efficient. Laguiole knives are classics and available in a mind-boggling array of shapes, sizes and colours.

~ P38 can opener ~
Aboveandbeyond.co.uk

You may have a can opener on your Swiss army knife, but you might just want one of these too. These were originally made in 1942 for the US military, to whom they were distributed as part of the daily combat food ration (known as the K ration). They are now much admired by kit aficionados for their simplicity, functionality and good looks and cost very little.

~ CAMPING & EXPLORING ~

~ Compasses ~
Telluricgroup.com

Unlike most other things here, I don't own a M-73 Leader's Compass, not least of all because they cost about £300. But I have seen them and want one; they are beautiful. They are also lightweight, robust and exceptionally accurate. The M-73 is made of brass with aluminium details (and some super-strength glass too, of course). Made by a specialist manufacturer founded in 1848, whose compasses were used by Dr Livingstone.

~ Fire blower/poker ~
Blowpoker.co.uk

These are a simple and useful cross between an ordinary poker and a bellows. The best we have come across is made by Blowpoker, a brass tube about 1m long and 2cm wide. You aim the blowpoker at the fire, blow and, hey presto! As the name suggests, the other end is a poker.

~ Folding shovel ~
Ecrater.co.uk

My dad used to carry a folding military shovel in his Land Rover and I loved it. I don't know why, particularly, but it was a thing of peculiar beauty to me. Recently I decided to buy myself something similar and did my research; all roads seemed to lead to the Chinese army PLA Survival Military Shovel WJQ-308. So, that's what I have; but a simple spade it is not. It is, in fact, a multifunction tool – the new Swiss army knife, even – good for digging, yes, but also for sawing, chopping, measuring, as a grappling hook, a pickaxe, for cutting up food, as a pair of pliers and much more.

~ First-aid kit ~
Bestmadeco.com

Every outdoor person needs a decent first-aid kit; we keep one in our Land Rovers and in our Airstream. Our favourite is by Best Made Company, not because its contents are any different to many other largish kits, but simply because it comes in the loveliest box imaginable. If you're going to display a first-aid kit, you might as well display an elegant one.

~ Handwarmers ~
thehotroxuk.co.uk

About a year ago we bought a rechargeable, electronic hand warmer by HotRox. Despite the naff name, this is a brilliant bit of kit for those who suffer from cold hands.

~ Torches ~
Maglite.com

Everyone needs a good torch in their life, especially if they plan to spend time in the countryside. For us there is only one classic torch: the Maglite. Maglite seems to have been around forever, but the company was, in fact, only founded in 1979, in California. Maglites come in a dizzying array of sizes and colours (too many, in my opinion). But the classic, black, 2D is the one for me; sleek, powerful, made of aluminium and with a variable focus beam. Perfection.

~ Headlamps ~
Snowpeak.com; Excellentstuff.com

Our friend Morven (RIP) used to wear a headlamp whenever she went camping or walking as a member of her very own Full Moon Club, and we used to laugh at her, because it looked so absurd. But we were wrong, headlamps are indispensable components of any camper's kit; we wish we could tell her. These are particularly useful when you are with small children; if they lose something you're free to search with both hands while also lighting your tent. The best I have ever seen is the lovely silicon SnowMiner Headlamp, which can quickly be converted into an efficient hanging lamp for your tent. When I asked around, the Stenlight 57 came up a couple of times, as the definitive headlamp (although you can buy quite a few SnowMiners for the price of one Stenlight 57).

~ Sleeping bags & sleeping bag rolls ~
Duluthpack.com; Marmot.com

There are loads and loads of great sleeping bags on the market and we seem to have amassed an industrial quantity, by endless different makers, at home. Therefore, it's hard for us to recommend one particular make, but lots of people we know swear by Marmot.

We have some sleeping bag rolls that are made by Duluth Pack in the US. Duluth is best known for its simple canvas backpacks but these rolls are brilliant. They are made of waterproof, breathable canvas; in spring, summer and autumn, slip your sleeping bag into one and you will be protected from damp and dew if you sleep outside the tent. In winter they add extra warmth inside the tent.

~ Match safes ~
Marblearms.com; Bestmadeco.com

Earlier in this book I talked about keeping your matches dry, or dipping them in varnish to protect them from the elements. But if you are a true outdoor person then I suspect you crave a serious bit of kit for storing your matches. There are loads of match safes – watertight containers that keep matches dry and also offer a striker – on the market and most of them are nasty plastic things. But this one is different; made by Marbles of Gladstone, Michigan, to a design patented in 1900 and pretty much unchanged ever since.

~ Storm Kettles ~
Kellykettle.com

Every good camper needs a Storm Kettle, otherwise known as a Kelly Kettle or Volcano Kettle; it is sort of a kettle and a campfire combined, fuelled by almost anything flammable you have to hand, such as twigs, paper or grass. They are biggish things, so only good for use near to your car or home. When I was a child my family had one of these that held me enraptured, for some reason, I think because it was so efficient at heating water, even in rain and wind. The smallest of twigs or bits of cardboard would result in boiling water in seconds. Kelly Kettles are still made in Ireland, where they have been manufactured for over 100 years.

~ Camp ovens ~
Lodgemfg.com

By far and away the best campfire oven we have ever had is an American camp oven (sometimes known as a Dutch oven) by Lodge (which we used to sell at Pedlars). This is a simple, very heavy, steel oven system, which is designed to be stacked on a campfire, one pot on top of the other. It is good for frying, stewing, warming, baking, roasting; you name it.

The idea is simple; you can use a small fire to cook a lot of different things. The largest pan sits in the embers and its lid is then piled with coals, onto which a smaller pan is placed; and so on. The system can also be used with a tripod. Lodge also make some brilliant, last-forever skillets and frying pans.

~ Stoves ~
Snowpeak.com; Coleman.eu;
Backpackinglight.co.uk

We have far too many camping stoves; a log-store overflowing with them, in fact. The best tiny stove we have is the Giga Power by Snowpeak, a really wonderful Japanese outdoor supplier. We also love our Coleman Unleaded Stove, which is a big, two-ring thing that runs on petrol. We think of the Coleman as the Land Rover of stoves. In the middle, size-wise, we have the Evernew Titanium stove, which we used for the first time last summer. This is, again, a Japanese design; Evernew have been making top-notch outdoor gear since the 1920s.

~ Tents ~
Wolfglentipis.co.uk; Belltent.co.uk; Pedlars.co.uk

Our favourite tent is our tipi. Simple canvas, natural rope and wood (we got ours from Wolf Glen Tipis). Next favourite is our European canvas bell tent. If you're after a really high-quality, performance tent, it's hard to beat the Helsport Varanger. We're new converts to these but can tell you that they look good, work well and combine aluminium with incredibly functional (fireproof, waterproof, lightweight) fibres. There are various sizes available and they can be supplied with an internal stove.

~ Whistles ~
Acmewhistles.co.uk

The Thunderer is, I think, the best whistle in the world; loud, elegant and made in Britain. Use it for alerting others to your whereabouts, or to danger, or even to raise the stubborn or hard-of-hearing after a picnic. Originally made by Joseph Hudson in Birmingham (which is where the company still manufactures, now under the name of Acme), these were first used by the Metropolitan Police in 1884.

~ Walking sticks ~
Your-adviser.com/bsg

We're not talking here about those carbon fibre poles with spiky bottoms that we have a little bit of a moan about earlier in this book (see p.54). We're talking about big, long, strong wooden sticks, maybe with horn tops; proper, old-fashioned sticks with flat bottoms that give you a sense of purpose and control. We have a huge collection of these, many of which were inherited, but lots of which we have collected ourselves. We have one with a pop-out pencil on the handle and we have a swordstick or two (if they are illegal, please don't tell anyone). We don't have a particular stickmaker to recommend, but if you're thinking about buying a stick, then the British Stickmaker's Guild is a good place to start your research. As they say, they're 'An organisation for stickmakers and collectors. Organised by stickmakers and collectors'.

~ Bheestie Bag ~
Bheestie.com

This is simple and brilliant; and every outdoor person should have one. If your phone or watch or whatever is wet, simply drop it into the Bheestie Bag and it'll do a fine job of drying it out. The manufacturers don't promise miracles but we have found this incredibly useful and efficient.

THE BEST MUSIC FOR THE GREAT OUTDOORS

Nigel House is the co-owner and manager of Britain's (or maybe the world's) best record shop, Rough Trade, which is right next door to our shop in Notting Hill. Everyone who works at Rough Trade knows and loves music; but Nigel knows the most and his enthusiasm is as genuine as it is infectious. Here are what Nigel considers to be the best records for the great outdoors.

~ The Kinks ~
The Village Green Preservation Society (Pye, 1968)

Sepia tinted pictures of a summer idyll that may or may not have ever existed. Perfection that personifies English towns and villages.

~ Ultramarine ~
United Kingdoms (Warner, 1993)

Robert Wyatt - surely the greatest living British vocalist - sings on two tracks of this almost perfect pastoral electronica.

~ The Unthanks ~
Last (Rabble Rouser, 2011)

Their best release so far with its mixture of minimalist production and pure vocal harmonies. With its roots in traditional folk, this travels far beyond that with its more varied instrumentation.

~ Van Dyke ~
Parks Discover America (Rykodisc, 1972)

A crazy mixture of calypso, country and exotica. Perfect for long sunny days.

~ Tom Russell ~
Hotwalker (Hightone, 2005)

If you ever drive down the west coast of the US, make sure you have this on the CD player - tales of grifters, Bukowski, Lenny Bruce, Kerouac and railways.

~ Leisure Society ~
The Sleeper (Willkommen, 2009)

Wistful and probably the closest we have to a modern Kinks. Blissful.

~ Van Morrison ~
Astral Weeks (Warner, 1968)

Could just have easily been Moondance - just such a great mixture of Irish tinged folk and jazz.

~ Robert Wyatt ~
Greatest Misses (Domino, 2004)

The only album on which you can find his version of Shipbuilding - Elvis Costello's best ever song.

~ Penguin Cafe Orchestra ~
Penguin Cafe Orchestra (EG Virgin, 1987)

Their second album, this is the English countryside laid down on record.

~ Paris, Texas ~
Original soundtrack (Warner, 1984)

Ry Cooder's finest soundtrack. Just listen to Harry Dean Stanton's voice. Perfection.

GOOD BOOKS FOR THE GREAT OUTDOORS

Jeff Barrett founded the legendary record label Heavenly Recordings, whose roster has included Doves, Manic Street Preachers, Beth Orton and The Magic Numbers. Jeff still runs Heavenly but also dedicates a lot of his time (and tireless enthusiasm) to Caught by the River, which he co-founded in 2007. Caught by the River is hard to define – it is a website, it publishes books and hosts events – but its mission is simple; to share knowledge and enthusiasm for nature, fishing, music, pubs, poetry, books, film, art, gardening and lots more besides. These are some of Jeff's favourite books about the great outdoors. *Caughtbytheriver.net*

~ Dart ~
Alice Oswald (Faber, 2002)

A homage to the River Dart. A fantastic, physical poem with a whole lot of soul.

~ The Lost Art of Walking ~
Geoff Nicholson (Harbour Books, 2010)

Don't be put off by the somewhat academic subtitle: The History, Science, Philosophy, Literature, Theory and Practice of Pedestrianism ! Unlike the other titles chosen here, the action is not exclusively 'country'. The author is an interesting guy, very hip, very informative and never boring.

~ Waterlog ~
Roger Deakin (Chatto & Windus, 1999)

A frog's eye view of the British Isles, written by the patron saint of Caught by the River. Pastoral anarchy.

~ Journey Across Britain ~
John Hillaby (Paladin, 1968)

A walk from Land's End to John o'Groats taken in 1966 by a man driven by curiosity. Hillaby purposefully avoided the main thoroughfares, sticking mostly to tracks and bridleways, getting himself into some terrifying situations on Dartmoor and the mountains of the Scottish Highlands for his troubles. A well-written book by someone with an eye for the offbeat.

~ A Lifetime of Mountains ~
A. Harry Griffin (Guardian Books, 2005)

Griffin spent his life in the Lakeland Fells. He was a *Guardian* country diarist for 53 years. This book is a selection from the diaries. He writes with a magnificent sense of place and adventure that have an effect on me made all the more credible by the fact that I have never even visited the region.

TEN MUST-READS ABOUT THE GREAT OUTDOORS

Freddie Baveystock is very clever indeed. He got a double first in English Literature at Oxford and then did a PhD. He is an enthusiastic walker, a music-nut and a DJ. He is also a voracious reader and the best person we know at making perfect recommendations of great books. We asked him to suggest his ten must-read books about the great outdoors.

The Oregon Trail
Francis Parkman (National Geographic, 1849)

Although educated at Harvard, and trained as a lawyer, young Parkman's interest in early American history and outdoors adventure became so obsessive that in 1846, at the age of 23, he travelled west to experience the last gasps of Plains Indian life for himself. A beautifully observed book in which a young man's yearning romanticism is filtered through a very beady, more discerning eye.

Great Plains
Ian Frazier (Granta, 1989)

Driven by a similar obsession to Parkman's, New Yorker writer Frazier spent a number of summers holed up in a Montana cabin, roaming around the now largely deserted Midwest. The result is a hugely evocative, irreverent yet heartfelt love song to an almost wholly vanished culture that makes more traditional approaches to history seem frankly dull.

Walden: or, Life in the Woods
Henry David Thoreau (Oxford World's Classics, 1854)

Thoreau's attempt to become self-sufficient during a period of rampant profiteering – not to mention slavery and warmongering – marked his card during his own time as a cantankerous freethinker. A disconcerting mix of prose poetry, punning wordplay and provocatively libertarian philosophy. Not everyone's cup of tea, for sure, but for adherents this is one of the touchstones of American literature as well as ecological thinking.

Teaching a Stone to Talk
Annie Dillard (HarperPerennial, 1982)

Dillard belongs to that ecstatic, almost mystical strain of nature writing that is such a vital element to the American tradition. This collection of short essays is perhaps the best way of experiencing it – like short nips of the purest malt whisky, each has a striking flavour and heady lucidity all of its own.

Great Two-Hearted River, The Collected Stories, 1925
Ernest Hemingway (Everyman's Library Collection)

Hemingway's early stories have a phenomenal purity of purpose, and perhaps none more so than this two-part tale of a solo camping trip in the wilds of Michigan into which he poured so much suppressed feeling and nuanced observation. A beautiful tribute to the restorative powers of nature.

A River Runs Through It
Norman Maclean (University of Chicago Press, 1976)

Yes, Robert Redford made the title story of this slim volume into a lushly romantic movie starring Brad Pitt, but don't let that put you off. The original account of the author's childhood in pre-war Iowa, in which fly fishing was an abiding solace, is so unsentimentally, yet lovingly written, it cannot but break your heart. It may also, like Hemingway's tale, make you want to take up fishing.

The Country of the Pointed Firs
Sarah Orne Jewett (Penguin Classics).
First edition, 1896

Ever a fiercely regional writer, this 1896 work is the apogee of Jewett's quiet, considered oeuvre. It is less than a novel than a work of atmosphere and environment, bringing to life the quiet life of a faded Maine coastal town, with all its buried passions and whispered tales. A subtle exploration of nature's power to make, break and re-make lives.

All the Pretty Horses
Cormac McCarthy (Picador, 1992)

McCarthy has a penchant for creating characters who are more at home in the world of cruel nature than in the infinitely more heartless world of their fellow men. His prose is extraordinary in its austere, almost Biblical sonority, effortlessly straddling the ages. This isn't his masterpiece – the monumental *Suttree* takes that honour – but it's probably his most immediately likeable book.

Crossing Open Ground
Barry Lopez (Picador, 1988)

One of the great scholar gentlemen explorers of modern American letters, Lopez will always be known for *Arctic Dreams*, a classic work that justly won the National Book Award. These essays are an excellent introduction to his work, showcasing the deftness with which he imparts his deep knowledge by weaving it around first-hand observation.

The Bear
William Faulkner. First published in 1942.
Now available as part of Three Famous Short
Novels (Vintage International)

Faulkner wrote an awful lot of tripe, which is justly neglected these days. This story, however, combines raw emotion with a more mythic quality – it's that old tale of paradise found and lost, or destroyed – which doesn't fade with time.

FURTHER READING

The Art of Manliness
Brett McKay (How Books)

Good further reading on chopping wood, and lots more too.

Finding Your Way Without Map or Compass
Harold Gatty (Dover Publications Inc)

In 1931 Gatty and Wiley Post flew around the world in a record-breaking eight days. So, he knew what he was talking about.

The Wilderness Route Finder
Calvin Rutstrum (University of Minnesota Press)

A classic – and a brilliant book for anyone who wants to get really serious about navigation. Originally published in 1967.

Knife Throwing: Sport..Survival..Defense
Blackie Collins (Knifeworld)

Woodlands
Oliver Rackham (Collins)

The 100th volume in the brilliant New Naturalist library, published by Collins. As thorough a guide to the British woodland landscape as you could hope for.

Bumblebees
Ted Benton (Collins)

Another excellent addition to Collins' New Naturalist series.

Climate and Weather
John Kington (Collins)

Again, part of the New Naturalist series.

Caught by the River: A Collection of Words on Water
Jeff Barrett, Robin Turner and Andrew Walsh (Cassell Illustrated)

On Nature: Unexpected Ramblings on the British Countryside
Caught by the River (HarperCollins)

The Scarecrow: Fact and Fable
Peter Haining (Robert Hale Ltd)

The English Village: History and Traditions
Martin Wainwright (Michael O'Mara)

Musson's Improved Lumber and Log Picket Book
(Lee Valley Tools, 2006 reprint)

Originally published in 1905.

The Forager Handbook
Miles Irving (Ebury Press)

Exhaustive, engaging.

Food For Free
Richard Mabey (Collins Gem)

This tiny guide includes photos and illustrations and is pretty much all you will need when foraging.

Mushrooms
Roger Phillips (Macmillan Reference)

An excellent reference guide to mushroom identification. Check out his website: *Rogersmushrooms.com*

Building a Wood-Fired Oven for Bread and Pizza
Tom Jaine (Prospect Books)

Wild Flowers
Sarah Raven (Bloomsbury)

Flora Britannica
Richard Mabey (Chatto & Windus)

A vast, thorough guide which offers a detailed survey of wild plants of England, Scotland and Wales.

Tiny Campsites
Dixe Wills (Punk Publishing Ltd)

Dixe (it's pronounced 'Dixie' in case you were wondering) shares his favourite very small, off-the-beaten-track campsites in Britain. Read his guide to campsite etiquette on p.142.

The Camping Cookbook
Annie Bell (Kyle Cathie)

Holiday
Bill Granger (Murdoch Books)

A travelogue with the emphasis firmly on food. See his recipes for chicken burgers with lemongrass and lime on p.224. and spicy slaw on p.231

Breakfast, Lunch and Tea
Rose Bakery (Phaidon)

Find inspiration for your picnic recipes.

No Guns, Big Smile: South America by Horse
James Greenwood (Michael Joseph)
Greenwood retraces the 5000-mile trek undertaken by the Swiss Long Rider and adventurer, Aimé Tschiffely, in the 1920s. Awesome-inspiring. Read about Greenwood's experiences of travel camping on p.138.

Primitive Technology: A Book of Earth Skills
From the Society of Primitive Technology. Edited by David Wescott (Black Sparrow Press)

Last Hours on Everest
Graham Hoyland (Collins)

What happened to George Mallory on his fatal bid to reach Everest's summit in 1924? Hoyland, also a mountaineer and a relative of one of the last men to see Mallory alive, returns to find out. Read his thoughts on outdoor clothing on p.158. A booklet about the Mallory Replica Clothing Project is available from the Mountain Heritage Trust. (*Mountain-heritage.org*)

The Cloudspotter's Guide
Gavin Pretor-Pinney, and his follow-up
The Cloud Collector's Handbook
(both published by Spectre)

Everything you could ever want to know about clouds without being scared by the science; by the co-founder of The Idler. Read about his favourite clouds on p.38 and visit his website: Cloudappreciationsociety.org

The Theory of Clouds
Stephane Audeguy (Harcourt Trade)

An offbeat read for those with an interest in clouds.

Beekeeping for Dummies
(Howell Dummies series)

Our beekeeping friend Pamela swears by this book (see p.76).

The Urban Beekeeper
Steve Benbow (Square Peg)

Founder of the London Honey Company's wonderful and inspiring story and his guide to keeping bees in the city.

FURTHER INFORMATION

- GREAT BRITISH WALKS -

CORNWALL: The Saint's Way
Cornwalls.co.uk/walking/the_saints_way.htm

CORNWALL: Port Isaac to Port Quin
Westcountrywalks.com/mid-se-cornwall/bodmin-ncoast/portisaac-portquin/portisaac-01.php

THE GRAMPIANS: The Mounth Roads
Tgomagazine.co.uk/walks/scotland/easthighlands/mount-roads
Walkscotland.com/walk151.htm

NORTHUMBERLAND/CUMBRIA/SCOTLAND: Hadrian's Wall Path
Hadrians-wall.org
Nationaltrail.co.uk/hadrianswall

THE HOME COUNTIES: The Ridgeway Path
Nationaltrail.co.uk/ridgeway
Stay at the Boar's Head pub, Church Street, Ardington, Wantage, Oxfordshire, OX12 8QA:
Boarsheadardington.co.uk

DERBYSHIRE: Dovedale, Ormaston and Alstonefield
Derbyshireuk.net/dovedale.html
Walkinginderbyshire.co.uk/ashbourne.htm
Derbyshire-peakdistrict.co.uk/index.htm

KINCARDINESHIRE: Clachnaben
Walkhighlands.co.uk/aberdeenshire/clachnaben.shtml

HEREFORDSHIRE: Black Hill/The Cat's Back
Bbc.co.uk/midlandstoday/content/articles/2009/01/14/catsback_herefordshire_140109_feature.shtml

HEREFORDSHIRE: Brecon Beacons National Park
Walkingbritain.co.uk/walks/walks/walk_list/Brecon_Beacons/

NORTHERN IRELAND: North Antrim Coast (and other walks)
Walkni.com
If you venture near Bushmills, stop for a pint of Guinness and some traditional Irish food at
The Nook, 48 Causeway Road, Bushmills, BT57 8SU (Tel: 028 2073 2993).

- RIDING HOLIDAYS -

GLOBAL
Ride Worldwide | *Rideworldwide.com* | Tel: +44 (0) 1837 82544
Adventurous riding holidays and horse safari tours abroad for experienced riders. Global destinations range from Ethiopia and France to India and North America. Variety of trip types, from family-friendly breaks to holidays combining yoga, riding and game-spotting (though not all at once).

WALES (Radnorshire)
Free Rein Riding Holidays | *Free-rein.co.uk* | Tel: +44 (0) 1497 821 356
Unguided 'door-to-door' riding through 'bracken covered ridges, mountain streams, old oak woodlands, conifer forests, rocky crags and heather moorlands' in the Cambrian mountains and Radnor hills. Guided rides and beginners' trails also offered.

WALES (Brecon)
Trans-Wales Trails | *Transwales.demon.co.uk* | Tel: +44 (0) 1874 711 398
Ride across windswept, rugged landscapes from the Black Mountains to the Irish Sea on an all-inclusive, family-run riding holiday. Weekend breaks and day rides for competent adult riders.

WALES (Llangorse Lake, Brecon)
Ellesmere Riding Centre | *Ellesmereridingcentre.co.uk* | Tel: +44 (0) 1874 658252
A small, family-run stables by the beautiful Llangorse Lake. Two- and five-day trails and pony treks on Ellesmere's Welsh and Irish cobs are available, if you are a reasonably competent rider.

WALES (Carmarthenshire)
Five Saints Riding Centre | *Fivesaints.com* | Tel: +44 (0) 1558 650580
Weekend breaks to summer camps and learn-to-ride holidays, in the unspoilt Cothi Valley. Bed and breakfast or camping in the secluded field attached to the farmhouse for non-riders too.

CUMBRIA
Stonetrail Holidays | *Stonetrailholidays.com* | Tel: +44 (0) 15396 23444
Luxury self-catering near the Lake District, whether you are riding or not. Day-only trips, but you can book horses for a private friends and family group hack, or build a day ride around a pub lunch. Riders must be 13 or over and able to trot for shorter rides, or canter for the longer ones.

SCOTLAND (Banffshire)
Tomintoul Riding Centre | *Highlandhooves.co.uk* | Tel: +44 (0) 1807 580210
Ride for as little as an hour or as much as six days, with a guide, through the spectacular scenery of the Cairngorm Mountains and Glenlivet Estate. Novice riders welcome, and there are different breeds according to ability.

To find out about more stables in different parts of the country, or locate a place where you can master the basics, try the British Horse Society, which has a fantastic online search resource. *Bhs.org.uk*

~ CYCLING TOURS ~

WALES: The Elan Valley, Powys, various routes
Hire your bikes from Clive Powell, who runs a local bike hire business: *Clivepowell-mtb.co.uk*. The company also organises 'Dirty Weekends', all-inclusive cycling mini-breaks for all abilities.

For more detailed route information, try:
Sustrans.org.uk/sustrans-near-you/wales/easy-rides-in-wales/elan-valley-trail-rhayader
(For fishing permits for the many dams along the Elan Valley route, Clive suggests the local angling club: *Rhayaderangling.co.uk*)

WARWICKSHIRE: Circular route starting and finishing at Stratford upon Avon
Hire your bikes from Ian Parkes of the Traditional Cycle Shop in Stratford upon Avon (and meet Ian and his team, Brum and DG) at: *Traditionalcycleshop.co.uk*

ESSEX: 25-mile circular route from Great Dunmow through The Rodings
Hire your bikes from Tim Gunn, who runs The Old Bicycle Company, near Great Dunmow, at: *Theoldbicycleshowroom.co.uk*. Tim is a lifelong local and knows the area inside out, so if you call ahead and warn him you're coming he'll be happy to help tailor-make a route for you and, if you're lucky, make you a cup of tea, too.

SCOTLAND: Cycle ride around Loch Katrine, which takes in a steamship trip
To find out more about the area, visit: *Lochkatrine.com*. And to hire one of Mark Shimidzu's bikes, go to: *Katrinewheelz.co.uk*

LONDON: Thames Path (and other tours)
For information on this and other guided bike tours, contact Graham Hills of Biker's Delight, at: *Bikers-delight.com*

~ MISCELLANEOUS ~

CONKER FIGHTING

The World Conker Championships happen each year, on the second Sunday in October at New Lodge Fields, Polebrook, near Oundle, Northamptonshire. Enter or find out more at *Worldconkerchampionship.com*

KETTLEWELL SCARECROW FESTIVAL

The Kettlewell Scarecrow Festival in North Yorkshire takes place each August. For more information go to: *Kettlewellscarecrowfestival.co.uk*

USEFUL BEE RESOURCES

British Beekeepers Association | *bbka.org.uk*

Welsh Beekeepers Association | *wbka.com*

Institute of Northern Ireland Beekeepers | *inibeekeepers.com*

Scottish Beekeepers Association | *Scottishbeekeepers.org.uk*

Thorn (for everything from budget beekeeping kits to useful addresses) | *Thorne.co.uk*

See also 'further reading' on p.258.

GROW YOUR OWN WALNUTS

Try the Walnut Tree Company at | *Walnuttrees.co.uk*

TROUT FISHING AND TICKLING

To find out where in Britain you can catch fish, and to obtain a rod licence (which it is illegal not to have when fishing) go to the Environment Agency's website and type 'where to go fishing' into the search box. | *Environment-agency.gov.uk*

Contrary to some opinions, trout tickling is not illegal. In fact, you don't even need a licence to do it, as fishing licences are for rods. However, there are a few rules about getting into rivers (which you can read about at: *Environment-agency.gov.uk*) and, in England and Wales, you would also need permission from whoever owns the riverbank in question.

Jeff Barrett
Freddie Baveystock
Jan Bowmer
Matt Blease
Pamela Brice
Mark Carleton-Smith
Archie Dykes
Audrey Dykes
Harry Enfield
Sir William Gladstone
Felix Gladstone
Xanthe Gladstone
James Graham-Stewart
Bill Granger
James Greenwood
Tim Gunn
Nigel Harvey
Catherine Hill
Graham Hills
Nigel House
Michael Kennedy
Ben Knight
Emily Mackie
Miranda McHardy
Ian Parkes
Andrew Pothecary
Clive Powell
Gavin Pretor-Pinney
Carol Price
David Price
Sally Sargeant
Gavin Screaton
Mark Shimidzu
Susan Smith
Pidge Spencer
Dixe Wills
Doug Kerr, Joe Bramall, Matt Saint, Gemma Germains and Tom Saxby at Mercy
Rose Davidson, Simon Rhodes, Tom Drake-Lee, Debbie McNally, Lee-Anne Williams, Kate Watson, Vicki Watson, Will Smith and Caroline McArthur at Square Peg and Random House

Charlie and Caroline Gladstone run Pedlars, an award-winning company selling 'wonderful stuff' for homes and the Great Outdoors. They are also organic farmers and own Hawarden Estate Farm Shop and The Glynne Arms in North Wales.

They have lived in the Highlands of Scotland for over twenty years. They have six children and lots of dogs, horses and chickens. With a long family history of outdoors expertise, anecdotes and unbridled passion, they are ideally placed to write this inspiring and irresistible guide to life beyond four walls.

Kate Burt met the Gladstones after writing a piece on them for the Independent, where she also writes a weekly interiors column in the Sunday magazine.

Matt Blease is an illustrator, designer and art director based in London.
www.mattblease.com

Mercy are a design agency with offices in both Liverpool and London. Established in 2006, they have been looking after the design and art direction for Charlie and Caroline's various businesses since 2010.
www.mercyonline.co.uk

Tim Winter first met Charlie and Caroline in 2001 when photographing them for a magazine feature at their home in Scotland. He has since worked with them to produce all Pedlars' photography, and has shot many further features with the family.
www.timwinter.co.uk

Text:
Headline - A2 Beckett, designed by A2/SW/HK
Body - Feijoa, designed by Kris Sowersby for the Klim Type Foundry